easy cycling

around vancouver

Jean Cousins and
Norman Cousins

GREYSTONE BOOKS

Douglas & McIntyre Publishing Group

Vancouver/Toronto

Greystone Books
A division of Douglas & McIntyre Ltd.
2323 Quebec Street, Suite 201
Vancouver, British Columbia
Canada V5T 4S7
www.greystonebooks.com

National Library of Canada Cataloguing in Publication Data

Cousins, Jean, 1928 –
   Easy cycling around Vancouver

   Includes index.
   ISBN 1-55054-897-2

   1. Cycling—British Columbia—Vancouver Metropolitan Area—Guidebooks. 2. Vancouver Metropolitan Area (B.C.)—Guidebooks. I. Cousins, Norman (Norman Francis). II. Title.
GV1046.C32V35 2002   796.6'4'0971133   C2001-911464-8

Editing by Lucy Kenward
Copyediting by Maja Grip
Cover photo by Sidney H. Rittenberg/firstlight.ca
Cover and text design by Sigrid Albert
Photos by Norman Cousins and Vi Wall
Maps by Eric Leinberger
Printed and bound in Canada by Friesens

Greystone Books is committed to reducing the consumption of old-growth forests in the books it publishes. This book is one step toward that goal. It is printed on acid-free paper that is 100% ancient-forest-free, and it has been processed chlorine free.

We gratefully acknowledge the financial support of the Canada Council for the Arts, the British Columbia Ministry of Tourism, Small Business and Culture, and the Government of Canada through the Book Publishing Industry Development Program (BPIDP) for our publishing activities.

Contents

Acknowledgements

Making this book was not a solo enterprise. We wish to thank all those who contributed their time and knowledge and encouraged us along the way.

In particular, we are indebted to Vi Wall for photographs and research; she proved once again that if you want something done you should ask a busy person. We thank Inge China for taking the trouble to make notes for us about cycle routes. We thank cycling friends Jean Hudson, Susan Rowe-Evans and Andrew Lyall for their company on rides and for patiently submitting to being photographed. We appreciate, too, the unknown cyclists encountered on our travels who were generous with local knowledge and good cheer. Personnel in visitor centres, museums and parks have readily shared their knowledge and experience. The editorial staff at Greystone Books have been on hand all along with encouragement and assistance.

We hope the finished product reflects these combined efforts and will give pleasure to the reader.

Elevated picnic spot

Introduction

This book is designed to encourage those who have wondered about taking up cycling—principally beginners but also families and older or perhaps "rusty" cyclists—but have been deterred by doubts as to how to go about it. Other books on cycling do exist, of course, and we acknowledge our debt to them. Those books first acquainted us with bicycle rides in southwestern British Columbia. Like many others, we were under the impression that we were familiar with the Fraser Valley because we had driven frequently from Vancouver to Hope on Highway 1. How wrong that impression was! Cycling has opened up countless villages, parks, riverside picnic spots and rural areas among lakes and mountains, all at a pace that is unique to cycling.

From that early introduction, and our own research over many years, we have compiled a collection of outings suitable to our preferred style. Readers of *Easy Hiking around Vancouver* will recognize that style—rides demanding enough to stretch your abilities while staying within the capabilities of most people.

Once you rid yourself of the notion that you must reach your destination in the shortest time possible, you can enjoy the stops—take a photograph, have a drink of water or smell the roses, as the fancy takes you.

It may also be helpful to clarify what our style of cycling is *not*. It is not competitive: you don't have to beat anybody else's time, not even your own. Nor do you have to adhere to a timetable. Further, cycling as we do it can hardly be described as a sport or a challenge, although effort does go into it and you might well feel its effects at the end of the day—tired limbs but better breathing!

The forty rides presented are short—between 10 and 45 kilometres. They are routed on paved roads or good gravel surfaces and avoid areas of heavy traffic as much as possible. Many are circular tours. You will notice that many of the rides are located in the Fraser Valley and northwestern Washington. We've tried to cover most areas around Vancouver in our collection, including Squamish to the north and Harrison to the east, but some parts of the Lower Mainland, though delightful, do not lend themselves to easy cycling. Similarly, we omit popular city cycle routes and paths (which are well covered in other books) not from disrespect but because they fall outside our category of countrified tours.

A descriptive summary precedes each ride, enabling you to find your level. A following paragraph gives an overview of the area or mentions places and facts of local interest. Sometimes optional routes or side trips are suggested. In most cases the recommended lunch stop offers a picnic table or bench, often in a park.

In another part of the book is practical advice on bicycles, equipment and clothing, with hints on comfort for the beginning and out-of-practice cyclist.

An important section on safety will help to reassure the fearful and encourage responsible cycling.

Perhaps some of our readers will be encouraged, after gaining experience and confidence from these rides, to try another approach to cycle touring. Many outdoor clubs organize group bike rides similar to those described in this book. Bicycle touring companies arrange and guide cycling holidays around the world. Call Cycling B.C. at 604-737-3034 for more information about related activities. For your bookshelf, the *Ultimate Bicycle Book*, by Richard Ballantine and Richard Grant (Willowdale, Ont.: Firefly, 1998) covers a range of topics, including bicycle history, touring and maintenance.

Don't be afraid to put together your own cycle tour, perhaps based on one or two of our rides in the Fraser Valley or Washington. Arm yourself with a map of your chosen area (International Travel Maps & Books at 539 West Pender or 530 West Broadway in Vancouver has a good selection—choose one with a scale of about 1:50,000) and pick out some secondary roads to link up with the routes in *Easy Cycling around Vancouver*. Arrange convenient overnight accommodation along the way, pack your panniers and set off. You will have embarked on a freewheeling style of holiday that knows no boundaries.

Cycling is fun, healthy, inexpensive and kind to the environment. Best of all, it lifts the spirit to travel at a leisurely pace, exploring the byways on a personal journey of discovery. Easy cyclists, like Robert Louis Stevenson, "travel not to go anywhere, but to go. [We] travel for travel's sake. The great affair is to move."

Foxgloves on riverbank near Agassiz

How to Use This Book

Map reading en route

We hope you will start by reading and becoming familiar with the following introductory chapters. Experienced cyclists may find the advice unnecessary, but novices will benefit from the recommendations, at least in the beginning.

Until you have some experience cycling, it is a good idea to begin with short and easy rides, building your confidence and ability until you can judge what you are capable of.

How do you choose a short, easy ride? At the beginning of every ride description is a list of features:

— **Round-trip distance.** The rides in this book range from 10 to 45 kilometres.

— **Terrain.** Routes mainly follow paved roads, but this section tells you if you will also encounter gravel dykes or shared footpaths and whether the ride is level or hilly.

— **Traffic volume.** We try to avoid busy roads, but it isn't always possible. Here we tell you how much car traffic to expect.

— **Time to allow.** The approximate length of time you will need for the round trip. It includes a lunch break of 30 minutes plus up to 30 minutes extra if there are unpaved roads, hills, etc. The range indicated—e.g., 2 1/2 to 3 1/2 hours—allows for riders' different paces.

— **Highlights.** We point out scenery and items of interest you may enjoy. This still leaves plenty for you to discover for yourself.

— **Picnic spot.** Whenever we can suggest a suitable spot for a picnic we do. Most sites fall about two-thirds of the way through the ride's total distance.

— **Starting point and how to get there.** We've tried to find places to leave your car that are easy to locate. Express buses from Vancouver to Surrey, Delta, Langley, Coquitlam, Maple Ridge and other suburban destinations all have bike racks that take two bikes. For transit information in the GVRD, contact TransLink (604-953-3333; www.translink.bc.ca). Greyhound buses to Abbotsford, Chilliwack and Mission do not have bike racks; bikes must be boxed and paid for as freight, and arrangements made in advance, which makes this option rather unworkable. The bus to Squamish and Whistler is an exception: it has a bike rack and there is a $5 charge. Call 604-482-8747 for schedule information.

Now that you know how to discover what is in a ride, you can begin to make choices.

The elapsed distances accompanying route instructions are meant simply to help identify turnings or alert you to points of interest. Due to a number of factors, these figures may not always be precisely accurate. Do not be dismayed if you come across minor discrepancies.

Our maps are intended as a guide to be used in conjunction with route instructions. We strongly recommend carrying a standard map of the area, such as the Rand McNally 1:28,000 series, at all times. If you get off course you'll find the complete picture helpful.

You might find it convenient to photocopy the route instructions and the map for easy reference on the ride. You can keep this handy in a pocket or on top of a handlebar bag. The rides are laid out on facing pages in the book, so they are easy to copy.

If you can, start early in the day before the roads become too busy. Note that on summer weekends the parks also can be very crowded.

You're ready to set out on your chosen ride. One thing will lead to another, and before long you'll discover for yourself other byroads to explore on your bicycle.

Bicycles and Equipment

Touring and Hybrid Bicycles

If you already own a bicycle, you'll probably want to use it for these rides, and who are we to say you shouldn't? However, some types of bike are more suitable for our purpose than others.

We prefer a "hybrid" bike, though you could also use a touring bike. Both of these are intermediate bikes (between the extremes of racing and mountain bikes) appropriate for our intermediate rides.

Racing bikes and mountain bikes were designed for purposes different from the leisurely meanderings we describe. But if you already own one of these types of bike, you can use it on these rides. Cycling these routes is enjoyable, no matter what your choice of bike.

About Bicycle Fitting

Many cyclists, including long-time owners, have not adjusted their bikes for proper efficiency. While this is not crucial for local shopping trips, you will notice the difference in comfort and safety on longer rides. The subject is too detailed to cover properly in this book, so in addition to the tips below ask for on-the-spot advice at a bicycle shop or refer to a book on bicycle maintenance.

Correct leg position at bottom of stroke

Bicycles are manufactured in various frame sizes for people of different stature. Once you've chosen a frame size, you can adjust the bike at several points to make it comfortable for you. For instance:

— Saddle posts can be moved up or down.

— Saddles can be moved backward or forward, and the front tilted up or down.

— Handlebars can be raised or lowered.

5

Your bike adjustments are correct if:

— When you sit on the bike, your leg is almost, but not quite, straight at the lowest point of your pedal revolution. Otherwise you are losing some of the downward force your legs are capable of producing.

— Your handlebars are within easy reach and your body is not angled forward too steeply for comfort.

— You are not slipping forward or backward on your saddle.

Getting these adjustments right is essential. If they are not correct, you will tire easily and be uncomfortable to the point where you will not enjoy cycling and might give it up. So it's worth taking the trouble to ensure that you are completely comfortable on your bike.

Bicycle Essentials and Accessories

Most touring and hybrid bikes come well equipped for touring, but those that aren't can easily be fitted with the desired equipment. Ideally, your bike should have:

Warning of approaching danger

Toe-clip

— **Medium tires.** A tire between 1 3/8 inches and 1 3/4 inches wide is suited to both paved roads and reasonably smooth gravel dykes. A slightly raised tread helps the tire grip on uneven surfaces.

— **Strong brakes.** Cantilever brakes are widely used and have strong pulling power.

— **Eighteen speeds or more.** A range of gears is good because it includes low ratios for hill climbing.

— **A rear-view mirror.** This is one of the most important safety accessories you can have. A medium to large mirror attached to the handlebars lets you see more than a tiny one attached to a helmet.

— **Mudguards.** When you're caught in a rainstorm, these tire protectors will prevent you from being soaked in the spray from your tires.

— **A rear luggage rack and panniers** (or just one). The metal rack bolts to your bike so that you can carry panniers. These can hold your rain gear, lunch, extra clothing, tools, countryside produce, etc. without upsetting your balance or being uncomfortably hot like a backpack. Let the bike carry your gear directly and you will never notice the weight. A bungee strap on top of your rack is a convenient way to hold articles of clothing you may want to slip on or off.

— **A handlebar bag.** This can carry items to which you want easy access, such as emergency tools, rags, energy rations, sunscreen, cash, a camera, maps and route instructions.

— **Toeclips.** These curved plastic or metal pieces fasten onto the front of your pedals to properly position your feet. Toeclips force you to put your weight onto the ball of your foot, which is the most efficient position for pedal power. Adjustable cloth or leather straps hold your feet in place. If you are a novice rider, delay fitting toeclips to your pedals until you feel totally comfortable on your bike. Always make sure the fasteners are loose enough to allow you to withdraw your shoes quickly when necessary, and remember to pull your feet backwards before dismounting.

— **A warning device**, most commonly a bell. A bell is required by law, and it is particularly useful to warn others on a shared pathway that you are approaching. Please do not ride at speed, ring your bell, then expect other users to avoid *you*.

— **A tool kit.** Buy a package of the basic tools you'll need to make simple adjustments.

Basic tools

— **A water bottle and carrier.** The metal or plastic cage fits on your bike frame and holds a water bottle. Drink often; dehydration can be a serious risk when you're exerting yourself.

— **A bicycle pump and a pressure gauge.** You may need to fasten the pump to the bike's frame with accessory clips obtainable at a bicycle shop. Make sure the pump fits the valve on your tube. Keep your tires properly inflated as noted on the side of the tires themselves.

— **A spare inner tube, tire levers and a patch kit.** Before you leave home, know how to change the tube; it's easier to repair the punctured one later than trying to mend it on the spot. The spare should be the same size as the original tube. It may come with either a Schraeder (fat) valve or a Presta (thin) valve—it doesn't matter which, except that it should be the same type as on the original tire.

— **A first-aid kit.** Unless you have special needs, a basic kit from the drugstore should see you through.

— **An anti-theft lock.** We recommend a U-lock for maximum strength. Otherwise keep your bike within sight at all times.

— **Lights.** These rides are intended to be done in daylight, but the law requires that you use a white front light and a red rear light if you'll be out past dark.

In addition, to make most of the trips in this book you will need a bicycle carrier for your vehicle. A variety of racks is available from bicycle and automotive retailers. (Note: lock your bike rack in the vehicle while you are out riding.)

Maintaining Your Bike

The following simple tasks will ensure your bicycle is safe and enjoyable to ride.

— Adjust brakes and periodically replace brake pads and cables.

— Properly position gear-change guides to prevent the chain slipping off the outside cogs.

— Lubricate and clean the chain.

Don't be put off by these maintenance duties. They don't need to be performed all that often, and if you aren't interested in doing them yourself bicycle maintenance shops will handle them for you. But they must be done by somebody, otherwise your bicycle will become unfit to ride.

Better yet, get a book on bicycle maintenance and become interested in what makes your bicycle work best.

A Suggested Wardrobe

Contrary to popular belief, you don't need to kit yourself out with expensive, specialized clothes—not, at any rate, for the type of cycling described in this book. Nevertheless, if that is what you fancy, the bicycle shops will be delighted to advise you.

Assuming that you'll undertake these rides from approximately April to October, you'll need to be prepared for weather ranging from cool to hot. The following should cover most eventualities:

— **Headgear.** Here you have no choice: the law in British Columbia requires you to wear a helmet. If you're not already a cyclist, you will have to buy a helmet certified by the Canadian Standards Association. Buy this at a bicycle shop and ask the staff to advise you on proper fit. A poorly adjusted or improperly secured helmet is itself a source of danger.

— **Layers for the upper body.** Try a T-shirt, a long-sleeved shirt, a sweater and a windproof and waterproof jacket (see rainwear). Outer layers can be pulled off as the day warms up. Bright colours will help passing traffic see you more easily.

— **Shorts.** These are our preferred legwear; we simply find them less restricting. To protect against saddle-soreness the seat needs to be padded, so you may have to get specially made cycling shorts or underwear for this purpose. You can also buy a padded saddle cover.

Equipped for easy cycling

— **Sneakers or athletic shoes.** We find these quite satisfactory provided they are not bulky, especially if you are using toeclips. Cleated cycling shoes are not a good idea for our kind of cycling, which includes walking about in parks or stores.

— **Rainwear.** You can't go out cycling without ever being caught in a shower, but again we suggest simple, lightweight rainwear. For comfort and safety, keep your torso dry with a waterproof jacket rather than a cape, which can billow in the wind and upset your balance. Waterproof pants are an option, but we find them uncomfortable against bare legs.

Cycling Safety

Cycling is not an inherently dangerous pastime. Popular opinion would like us to believe that we risk our lives when we venture onto the roads. Not so. The statistics suggest that cycling fatalities are among the lowest of many categories of activity.

Nonetheless, cycling safety requires more than the donning of a helmet, which, as manufacturers warn, provides no protection to parts of the body that it does not cover. All cyclists can substantially reduce the possibility of accidents by following a few tried and true guidelines for minimizing cycling risk.

— Keep well to the right of the road, out of the way of overtaking traffic.

— Cycle in single file when travelling with others. Cycling abreast increases risk to the outside rider and makes it more difficult for a driver to pass safely. Yes, we know that cycling in single file inhibits conversation, but it reduces risk.

— Leave 3 to 4 metres between you and the cyclist ahead of you, and don't allow another rider to follow closely behind you. A sudden stop or a change of direction by either one of you can cause a collision, knocking both of you off your bikes.

Right

— Check your rear-view mirror frequently. Advance notice of traffic approaching from behind—including hell-bent cyclists—reduces surprises and consequently saves you from accidents.

— When riding downhill, raise your body slightly off the saddle to shift more weight onto the pedals. This, combined with the suppleness of your knees, gives you much better control over your bicycle if you hit a bump or other irregularity at speed. Resist the temptation to let loose on the downward grade; keep your speed

Wrong

11

to the point where you know you can brake to a full stop within the distance you can see. If you go too fast into a blind bend, you might swing over to the far side of the road into oncoming traffic.

— Approach left turns with great care. Make your intentions clear by signalling with your arm. Move towards the middle of the road and make your turn when it is safe to do so. Don't ride across the path of oncoming traffic. If traffic is heavy, be prepared to dismount and walk your bicycle across two sides of the intersection. In short, you can't be too careful when turning left at busy intersections.

— Dismount and walk your bike across oblique railway tracks. If you want to ride across them, ensure that there's no road or rail traffic approaching the crossing from any direction. If there is, stop until it has passed. From a short distance back, ride to a position where you are facing the tracks at a 90-degree angle. Cross the tracks straight on and resume your ride on the right side of the road.

— Wear an eyeshield, preferably a slightly tinted wide-angle shield that will not impair your range of vision. If you cycle often, something—dust, insects, small pebbles—will from time to time fly into your eyes, possibly resulting in a fall. A light plastic shield will usually provide protection against this.

— Practise dismounting rapidly so that you can do this instinctively and safely if you must stop in a hurry.

— Keep an eye out for dogs, and stay calm when they appear without warning. Try not to brake suddenly or swerve. Often, the stern command "Stay!" will deter a chasing dog. In our experience it is best to keep going; when you leave its territory, the dog will usually give up.

— Be watchful when passing parked cars. A door could be opened into your path.

— Be a responsible road user. Obey road rules, including stop signs and red lights. Do not ride on sidewalks except where specifically allowed. Even then, give pedestrians the right of way and pass them only at low speed.

— On dykes and trails, expect to meet walkers, dogs (which should be on a leash but often aren't), children, horses (which can be nervous) and other cyclists. Remember that most of these users have the right of way over cyclists. Please help to uphold the good reputation of cyclists by keeping speed to a minimum and generally respecting the rights of other users.

Your safety is not a matter of chance; it is overwhelmingly in your own hands. Recognize the risks and what you can do to reduce them. Then, irksome though you may find them at first, follow these rules. By doing so, you reduce the risks of cycling because you put yourself deliberately in control.

In conclusion, we repeat that the first rule of cycling safety is to ride well to the right of the road in single file. Nothing else ranks in importance with this golden rule. It maximizes your chance of staying out of trouble every moment of every ride.

"Stay!"

Key to Maps

——— Bike route on road
- - - Bike route on trail
▤ Highway
— Road
- - - - Other trail
+—+—+ Railway
⊔⊔⊔ Dyke
ⓟ Parking
☐ ⊼ Park, Picnic Area

Index Map

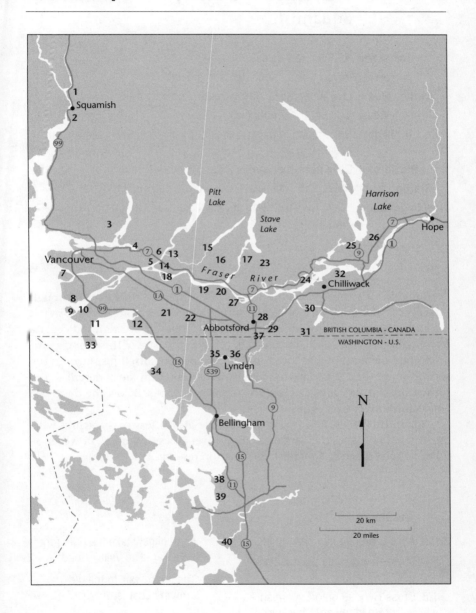

1 Paradise Valley
Squamish

Round trip	15.8 km (10 miles)
Terrain	Paved roads; some flat, some gentle hills
Traffic volume	Low on Paradise Valley Road, moderate around Hwy 99
Allow	1 1/2 to 2 1/2 hours
Highlights	Quiet roads, mountain views, Cheakamus River, old-growth cedar
Picnic spot	Dyke near Cheakamus River bridge at 7.9 km
Starting point	Alice Lake Provincial Park day-use parking lot
How to get there	Leave Hwy 99 North at Alice Lake sign, 10 km north of Squamish.

Camping at Alice Lake? For a change of pace from park trails, try this short foray into secluded Paradise Valley.

After crossing the Cheakamus River in Cheekye, the road winds through typical coastal forest, much of it environmental reserve. Along the way, watch for an unobtrusive sign leading to a thousand-year-old western red cedar a few metres from the road. A boardwalk protects the base of this living giant.

A good picnic spot and turnaround point presents itself just beyond the second bridge at 7.9 kilometres, where an information kiosk describes the formation and action of glaciers, rivers and volcanoes. Below the dyke, the Cheakamus River sweeps around a gravel bar.

Squamish Valley Road west of Cheekye also offers easy cycling with breathtaking views of the Tantalus Range. River access is limited, however, as the road runs through Squamish First Nation reserves.

The Route

km 0.0 Alice Lake day-use parking lot. Proceed down the park access road to Hwy 99.

1.3 Cross Hwy 99 onto Squamish Valley Road toward Cheekye.

4.8 Cross the Cheakamus River bridge at Cheekye and immediately take the right fork onto Paradise Valley Road.

6.2 The boardwalk to the old-growth cedar is on your left.

6.9 Keep straight on past North Vancouver Outdoor School and road to Evans Lake.

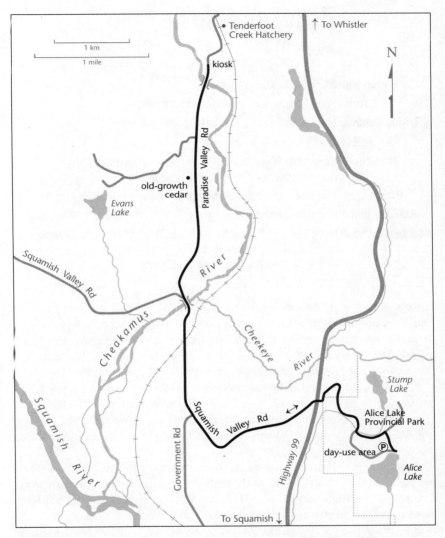

7.9 Bridge across Cheakamus River. The information kiosk and picnic spot are ahead on your left.

Option: For a self-guided tour of Tenderfoot Creek Fish Hatchery, continue north for 2 km. The road becomes gravel shortly beyond that point.

7.9 Return south on Paradise Valley Road.

11.0 Left on Squamish Valley Road to cross the river in Cheekye.

14.5 Cross Hwy 99 and continue up the Alice Lake Park access road.

15.8 Alice Lake day-use parking lot.

2   Brackendale
Squamish

Round trip	21.5 km (13 1/4 miles)
Terrain	Paved roads with optional dirt trail; flat
Traffic volume	Low except for downtown Squamish
Allow	2 to 3 hours
Highlights	Squamish River, Brackendale Eagles Provincial Park, Brackendale Art Gallery, mountain views
Picnic spot	Riverbank or beach at the end of Brennan Road at 10.9 km
Starting point	Visitor Information Centre on Cleveland Avenue in Squamish
How to get there	From Hwy 99 North, turn left (west) at the Cleveland Avenue traffic lights into Squamish and follow Cleveland Avenue to the visitor centre, south of Victoria Street.

Squamish lies at the foot of a granitic monolith, at the confluence of three major rivers and at the head of a fjord. The rugged landscape, a mecca for mountain bikers and rock climbers, might seem daunting to the "easy" cyclist, but there are quiet, level roads through the Squamish/Mamquam flood plain that provide peaceful riding with stunning mountain views.

Breeze out to Brackendale, the notorious "squamish" wind at your back, pausing at Eagle Run, where from November to February each year thousands of bald eagles gather to feed on spawned-out salmon. On the dyke, a log shelter decorated by Sko-mish First Nation carvers houses interpretive panels on eagle lore.

Perhaps eight thousand years ago, the ancestors of this region's Sko-mish people arrived at Howe Sound at the end of an unimaginable journey from Asia by way of the Bering Strait, Alaska and the west coast. Millennia later came explorers, fur traders and gold seekers and, eventually, non-Native settlers to make their home in the valley. By 1890 Brackendale was the site of the Squamish Valley Hop Company, a thriving regional industry until it was overtaken by forestry and tourism.

If you're staying in Squamish and fancy a day out of the saddle, you could explore the network of walking trails around the estuary, visit Railway Heritage Park to look over Canada's largest collection of rolling stock, or simply watch B.C. Rail's *Royal Hudson* steam train chug into town from North Vancouver.

Sign for optional route

DISCOVERY TRAIL
Celebrating Squamish Trails

↑ 1.3 km Industrial Way
1.9 km Dentville
2.7 km Youth Centre
3.3 km Cleveland Ave.

Please Keep Clean

SQUAMISH TRAILS SOCIETY
TOGETHER ON TRAILS

District of Squamish

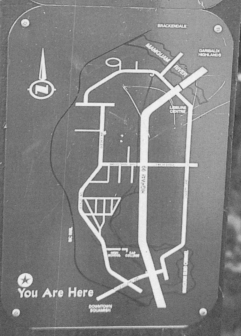

BRACKENDALE

MAMQUAM RIVER

GARIBALDI HIGHLANDS

LEISURE CENTRE

HIGHWAY 99

★ You Are Here

DOWNTOWN SQUAMISH

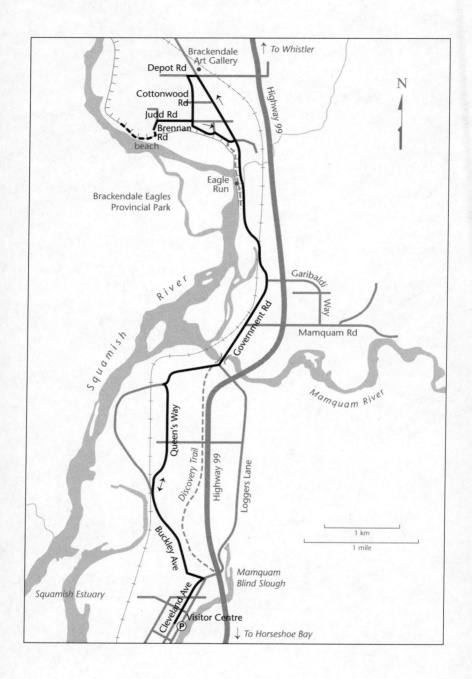

The Route

km 0.0 From the Visitor Information Centre, go north on Cleveland Avenue. Observe four-way stops on this busy main street.

0.9 Left onto Buckley Avenue immediately after the railway tracks. Buckley becomes Queen's Way through the industrial area.

4.1 Right on Government Road. Left leads to Railway Heritage Park.

5.0 Left on Government Road, following the sign to Brackendale and crossing Mamquam River bridge.

7.7 Opposite Easter Seal Camp is Brackendale Eagles Provincial Park. The log shelter is on the dyke.

9.2 Brackendale Store and Café on your left.

9.5 Left on Depot Road. To visit Brackendale Art Gallery continue a few metres farther on Government Road—look for the unicorn.

9.6 Left on Cottonwood Road.

10.2 Right on Judd Road.

10.7 Left on Brennan Road at sign "River Access."

10.9 Squamish River. From the dyke top a track left leads down to a sandy beach. Or picnic on rocks overlooking the river where the dyke path bends.

Shelter at Eagle Run

10.9 Backtrack on Brennan Road.

11.1 Right on Judd Road.

11.6 Right on Maple Crescent.

11.9 Right on Eagle Run Drive.

12.2 Right on Government Road.

15.5 Cross the Mamquam River bridge and go right on Government Road.

Option: Those riding mountain bikes can return to Squamish via Discovery Trail. See the signpost and map on the south side of Government Road at this point. Otherwise, continue on Government Road, which becomes Queen's Way and then Buckley Avenue.

19.6 Right on Cleveland Avenue and cross the railway tracks.

21.5 Visitor Information Centre.

3   Seymour Valley

Lower Seymour Conservation Reserve
North Vancouver

Note: The construction of a paved recreational trail roughly parallel to the Seymour Mainline is in progress at the time of writing. It is expected to open in spring 2002 and will then be available to hikers, cyclists and in-line skaters throughout the week. The parking lot will also be relocated. These improvements will enhance, without substantially changing, the outing described here.

Round trip	22 km (13 3/4 miles)
Terrain	Paved road; a few hills
Traffic volume	Only hikers, in-line skaters and other cyclists
Allow	2 to 3 hours
Highlights	Coastal forest, wildlife, views of Mount Seymour and Coliseum Mountain, Seymour Falls Dam and Seymour Lake, Seymour River Hatchery, Old Growth Trail (optional side trip)
Picnic spot	Seymour River Hatchery at 11 km
Starting point	Rice Lake Gate parking lot (or new location)
How to get there	Leave Hwy 1 in North Vancouver at exit 22 and drive north on Lillooet Road to its end at Rice Lake Gate.

It is a rare pleasure to ride a bicycle (comfortably) into a wilderness area where forest, river, mountain and wildlife are close at hand. The Seymour Mainline/recreational trail travels 11 kilometres into the glacier-carved Seymour River Valley.

The Lower Seymour Conservation Reserve is a working forest in what was once closed watershed land. Since being opened for recreation in 1987, the area has been carefully managed to ensure the water supply is available for future use, if that should become necessary. The area is largely second-growth forest; remnants of old corduroy roads and wooden pipelines attest to earlier logging operations. The reserve is home to deer, bears, cougars and other animals. It is always a thrill to encounter wildlife, but play safe by keeping your distance. *Never* attempt to feed or touch a wild creature.

The Seymour Falls Dam was built in 1961 to supply drinking water to the Lower Mainland. From the top of the road you can look through the fence at the 20-kilometre-long reservoir. A wooden platform lower down provides a view of the spillway and the Seymour River.

After a picnic at the Seymour River Hatchery, lock up your bike and walk the 1.7-kilometre loop trail beside Hurry Creek to see a magnificent stand of old-growth trees. Boardwalks make passage easier among the streams and rain-forest tangle. The trail begins at the bridge below the hatchery.

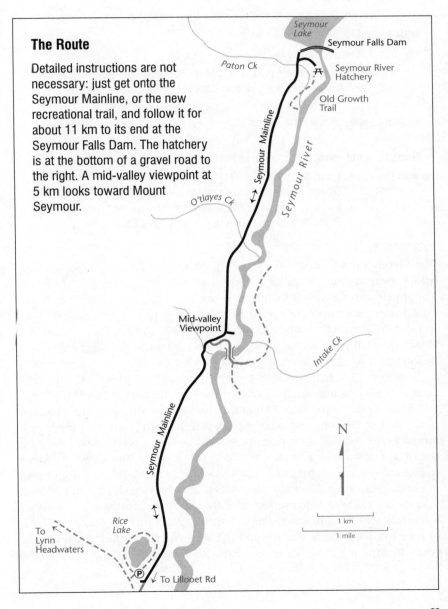

The Route

Detailed instructions are not necessary: just get onto the Seymour Mainline, or the new recreational trail, and follow it for about 11 km to its end at the Seymour Falls Dam. The hatchery is at the bottom of a gravel road to the right. A mid-valley viewpoint at 5 km looks toward Mount Seymour.

Seymour Lake

Seymour Falls Dam

Paton Ck

Seymour River Hatchery

Old Growth Trail

Seymour Mainline

Seymour River

O'tlayes Ck

Mid-valley Viewpoint

Intake Ck

N

Seymour Mainline

Rice Lake

To Lynn Headwaters

1 km

1 mile

P To Lillooet Rd

4   Sasamat Lake
Port Moody/Anmore

Round trip Up to 18 km (11 1/4 miles)

Terrain Paved roads and unpaved cycle path; some flat, some hills

Traffic volume Low to moderate

Allow 2 to 3 1/2 hours

Highlights Rocky Point Park and Station Museum, Shoreline Park, views of Burrard Inlet, Noons Creek Hatchery, Old Orchard Park, Sasamat Lake

Picnic spot White Pine Beach at 9 km (or Old Orchard Park on outward or return leg)

Starting point Rocky Point Park in Port Moody

How to get there From St. Johns Street in Port Moody, turn left on Moody Street. Follow the overpass around to the left, and turn left at the stop sign onto Murray Street. The parking lot for Rocky Point Park is just beyond the Station Museum.

Port Moody's designated bike routes, by their very nature, take the cyclist's breath away, as they lie among the rolling hills surrounding Port Moody Arm. By beginning with the gentle 3-kilometre cycle path in Shoreline Park, cyclists have the option of turning around at the end of Alderside Road or Ioco School or simply lazing away the day in Old Orchard Park. Others can accept the challenge and reap the reward of a picnic at Sasamat Lake, with the bonus of some free-wheeling on the way home.

Shoreline Park is a precious stretch of waterfront preserved for recreational use—a commendable feat in a development-crazed society. A trail and boardwalks for pedestrians hug the shoreline. Running roughly parallel to the pedestrian trail, the cycle path passes through coniferous forest and mixed woodland with occasional views of the tidal flats. Cyclists can walk their bikes down to the mouth of Noons Creek, where unearthed middens indicate this was once the site of Native encampments. There are glimpses of Burrard Inlet from Alderside Road, albeit from between waterfront homes.

Sasamat Lake, in Belcarra Regional Park, is often thronged on summer weekends, when families come out to picnic and swim at White Pine Beach or hike the 3-kilometre trail around the lake. At other times you may find yourself with only the birds and squirrels for company.

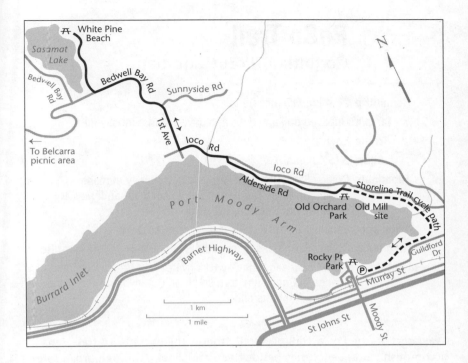

The Route

km **0.0** Parking lot for Rocky Point Park. Pick up the designated cycle path and proceed in an easterly direction. Side trails lead to Noons Creek Hatchery, Old Mill site and viewing platform.

3.0 Old Orchard Park. Picnic tables, toilets, beach.
Continue west along Alderside Road.

4.8 Left onto loco Road. Some gentle ups and downs.

5.6 Right on 1st Avenue, opposite the church. loco School is on the corner. Begin a gradual climb.

6.4 Keep left on Bedwell Bay Road toward Belcarra where Sunnyside Road forks right.

There are some bends and steep hills, but a wide shoulder to cycle on.

7.8 Right to White Pine Beach. Ride the gentle downhill to the beach.

9.0 Left into the first parking lot and walk bikes down the trail to the beach. Picnic tables, toilets, swimming, concession on summer weekends.

9.0 Retrace your outward route via Bedwell Bay Road, 1st Avenue, loco Road, Alderside Road and the Shoreline Park cycle path.

18.0 Rocky Point Park. Picnic area, toilets, pier. The Station Museum records Port Moody's railway history.

5　PoCo Trail

Coquitlam/Port Coquitlam

Round trip 27.4 km (17 miles)

Terrain Unpaved trail and dyke and paved roads; mostly flat

Traffic Low

Allow 3 to 4 hours

Highlights Colony Farm Regional Park and community gardens, Coquitlam River, Reeve and Lions Parks, urban forest, Hyde Creek Nature Reserve, Pitt River

Picnic spot Benches on the Pitt River dyke after 15.9 km

Starting point Colony Farm parking lot at the south end of Colony Farm Road

How to get there From Lougheed Highway (Hwy 7) east of Cape Horn interchange in Coquitlam, turn south on Colony Farm Road and drive 1.2 km to its end.

Wayfarers on the PoCo Trail need only follow the well-placed trail signs to accomplish a unique journey beside rivers and creeks, through urban forest and neighbourhood parks.

The brainchild of Pitt River swing-bridge operator Harold Routley, the idea of a trail that would encircle the City of Port Coquitlam captured the imagination of the community. Enthusiastic supporters were soon blazing the way with machetes and shovels. As the project grew, local, provincial and federal governments lent their aid; the trail was completed in 1974, its maintenance turned over to Port Coquitlam Parks and Recreation soon after.

Improvements and changes to the trail continue to be made when necessary—a new section along the Mary Hill By-pass is under construction at the time of writing—but the PoCo Trail is here to stay. Just follow the signs.

Note: Since the De Boville Slough dyke—also part of the PoCo Trail—is included in another ride (see page 30), we've taken a shortcut here. Purists can, of course, cycle every inch of Harold Routley's dream.

On the PoCo Trail

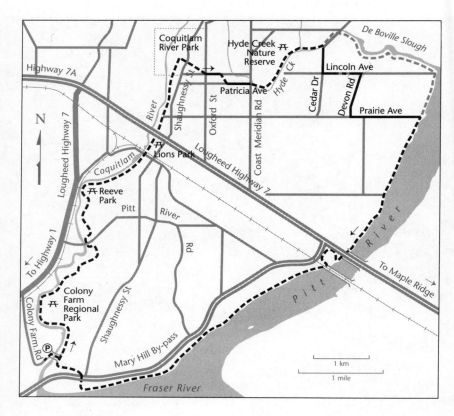

The Route

km 0.0 Colony Farm parking area. Leave the car park by the multi-use trail at the southwest corner of the lot, not by the path designated for walkers.

0.7 Right over the bridge across the Coquitlam River, then left on Wilson Farm Dyke Trail.

1.3 Straight ahead where Pumphouse Trail joins on the right. Watch for coyotes on Colony Farm lands.

2.7 Left at the fork—follow PoCo Trail signs from now on.

4.1 Pitt River Road. Do not cross the road, but follow signs left and through the underpass, then right to the car park on the west side of the road.

4.4 A paved section of trail begins at the top of the car park.

5.3 Reeve Park. Follow the trail around the sports field. Continue left. Pass under the railway and into Lions Park. Interpretive panels describe the history of PoCo Trail. Cross Lougheed Highway via the underpass. Keep left where the pavement ends.

Coquitlam River, Colony Farm

8.8 Follow the PoCo Trail sign right, up the incline. Keep left after crossing the creek.

9.3 Cross Shaughnessy Street and re-enter the woods.

9.8 Cross Oxford Street, then go left on Lincoln Avenue. Pick up PoCo Trail entering the woods on your right.

10.3 East along Patricia Avenue. Cross Coast Meridian Road and pick up the trail opposite. Enter Hyde Creek Nature Reserve.

12.5 Leave PoCo Trail and begin a shortcut by going right on Cedar Drive where PoCo continues left to cross the creek.

13.1 Left on Lincoln Avenue to Sun Valley Park. Go through the wire fence and walk straight ahead across the grass to continue on Lincoln Avenue.

13.8 Right on Devon Road at the stop sign.

14.6 Left on Prairie Avenue.

15.9 Right on Pitt River dyke to rejoin the PoCo Trail. There are good lunch spots along here with views of the Golden Ears.

18.7 Follow PoCo sign left to go under the bridges. Follow PoCo and bicycle signs carefully through this complicated section with several changes of direction.

20.3 Right on dyke path at top of incline. Industrial premises on right. Next to the Norco building is a rose garden with benches.

22.9 Gillnetter Pub. Follow PoCo Trail through this newly completed section.

25.6 Shaughnessy Street. Cross Mary Hill By-pass on the pedestrian crosswalk and pick up PoCo on the west side of Shaughnessy to re-enter Colony Farm Regional Park.

26.7 Cross Coquitlam River and go left on the west side.

27.4 Colony Farm parking area.

6   De Boville Slough
Coquitlam/Port Coquitlam

Round trip	17.2 km (10 3/4 miles)
Terrain	Paved roads, gravel dyke paths and trail; flat
Traffic volume	Low, except on Prairie Avenue
Allow	2 to 3 hours
Highlights	Pitt River, De Boville Slough, Minnekhada Regional Park, Hyde Creek and PoCo Trails
Picnic spot	Minnekhada Regional Park at 10.5 km or Addington Lookout
Starting point	Cedar Drive Park on Prairie Avenue
How to get there	From Lougheed Highway (Hwy 7) drive north on Coast Meridian Road. Turn right onto Prairie Avenue and drive for about 1 km to the small park on the right.

Ten kilometres of dyke top and trail help to make this a safe and interesting family ride. The circuit is short, but there is much to see and do. Budding naturalists will spot herons and waterfowl in the marshes bordering De Boville Slough, ospreys over the Pitt River and muskrats sliding into the water from their muddy holes. In September, you might see chum salmon heading up the slough to spawn in Hyde Creek. Binoculars are useful on this ride.

The climb to Addington Lookout could be a popular option, rewarding the energetic with a grand view across Addington Marsh and the Pitt River to the Golden Ears. For a less challenging lunch spot, wheel into Minnekhada Regional Park where picnic tables and other facilities are at hand. Hiking trails encircle the marsh and ascend the park's two rocky knolls. Minnekhada Lodge, once part of the private domain of B.C.'s lieutenant-governors, is open to the public most Sunday afternoons.

After a short stretch on Cedar Drive the route joins Hyde Creek Trail, part of the PoCo Trail system encompassing the area between the Coquitlam and Pitt Rivers. Cycling the wide gravel track through stately forest, you'll reach the Hyde Creek Recreation Centre—a mere 1.3 kilometres from your starting point on Prairie Avenue.

Lone rider on Pitt River dyke

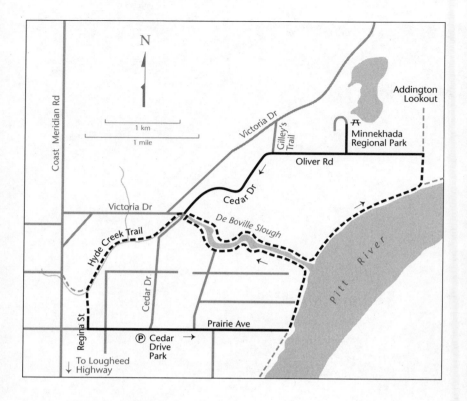

The Route

km 0.0 Cedar Drive Park. Right (east) on Prairie Avenue.

2.1 Left onto dyke path. Cycle first along Pitt River then along De Boville Slough.

5.2 Turn right on Cedar Drive and right again onto the dyke path on the north bank of De Boville Slough. The path veers away from the water then continues along Pitt River.

9.1 Left after farm gate and continue straight ahead toward Minnekhada hill.

9.5 Option: Straight ahead on the dyke leads to a footpath up to Addington Lookout. Lock your bicycle before climbing. Otherwise, go left at the gate onto Oliver Road.

10.2 Right between gateposts to Minnekhada Regional Park.

10.5 Bend in driveway: picnic tables, bike rack, toilets. Minnekhada Lodge is up the hill at the end of the driveway.

10.5 Return along the driveway.

10.8 Right on Oliver Road. Minnekhada Farm is on the right, now being restored.

Keep straight ahead on Cedar Drive.

Pitt River

13.8 De Boville Slough gate. Go
straight across the intersection
onto the signposted Hyde
Creek Trail.
After the bridge continue right
on PoCo Trail.

15.9 Hyde Creek Recreation Centre
parking lot. Head left past the
front of the recreation centre
building and join the running
track on the east side of the
field. Go through the wire fence
onto Regina Street.

16.5 Left on Prairie Avenue. Use the
crosswalk at this intersection if
necessary.

17.2 Cedar Drive Park.

7   Iona Island
Richmond

Round trip	18.7 km (11 1/2 miles)
Terrain	Paved road and unpaved service road; flat
Traffic volume	Low
Allow	1 1/2 to 2 1/2 hours
Highlights	Ocean and river views, beach, Iona jetty, McDonald Beach Park
Picnic spot	Iona Beach Regional Park at 13.4 km
Starting point	McDonald Beach Park
How to get there	From Grant McConachie Way (the approach road to Vancouver Airport's main terminal), turn right on Templeton Street, left on Grauer Road and right on McDonald Road.

For many urban cyclists, a quick way to get out in the open with a bike is to skirt Vancouver Airport and head for Iona Island. Some may be able to cycle from home to this destination, or transport their bicycles by car or bus as far as Templeton Street, just off Grant McConachie Way. For the short and easy ride described here, a convenient place to start and finish is McDonald Beach Park, which offers a concession, shaded picnic tables on the riverbank and lively boating activity to watch.

McDonald Beach Park

Situated at the mouth of the North Arm of the Fraser River, Iona Beach Regional Park comprises riverbank, marsh, tidal flats and a long sandy beach backed by grassy dunes. A service road alongside a 4-kilometre-long pipeline carrying treated sewage out to sea provides cyclists with an unusual sea-level ride with a nautical bias.

Iona is an important stopover on the Pacific Flyway, attracting thousands of migrants in spring and fall and many keen birdwatchers year-round. The island is usually breezy so make sure you have windproof clothing.

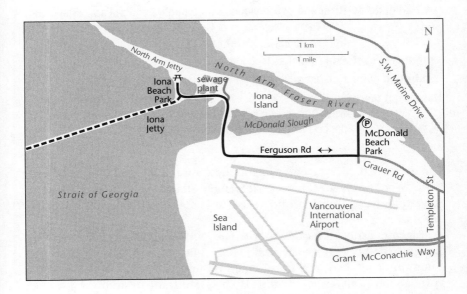

The Route

km 0.0 McDonald Beach Park.

0.8 Right on Ferguson Road.

3.3 Causeway linking Sea Island and Iona Island. McDonald Slough is on your right.

4.2 Left to Iona Beach Regional Park. Pipeline from sewage treatment plant alongside road.

5.1 Left on Iona jetty at the information kiosk. Cyclists must use the service road, not the walkway on top of the pipe.

9.1 Jetty terminus. View from the platform of the North Shore mountains and Vancouver Island.

9.1 Backtrack along the jetty.

13.1 Left on road.

13.4 Parking lot and South Marsh. Toilets, beach access and picnic tables.

13.4 Retrace your outward route.

18.7 McDonald Beach Park.

8   Richmond South Dyke
Richmond

Round trip	20.4 km (12 3/4 miles)
Terrain	Paved road and unpaved path; flat
Traffic volume	Low, except in Steveston
Allow	2 to 3 hours
Highlights	River and ocean views, Finn Slough, London Farm, Steveston wharf and village, Gulf of Georgia Cannery, Garry Point, Scotch Pond
Picnic spot	Garry Point at 10.5 km
Starting point	Horseshoe Slough parking lot on Dyke Road
How to get there	Leave Hwy 99 at exit 32 and drive west on Steveston Highway. Turn left on No. 5 Road and right on Dyke Road. The parking area is on the right after 0.3 km.

There is no better way to enjoy Richmond's South Dyke Trail than by bicycle. From Woodwards Landing at Horseshoe Slough Trail's eastern end to Steveston's heritage waterfront, a succession of interesting scenes and places unfold.

Tugs and fishboats bustle about on the south arm of the Fraser River. Finn Slough (seen on your return route) is the relic of an 1890s Finnish fishing community, its sheds and houses built on pilings. Farther west, you could visit London Farm or the Britannia Heritage Shipyard, or simply follow your nose, and South Dyke Trail signs, to Steveston village. Make your way to the public wharf to browse among gift shops, sample tasty Japanese snacks or buy fresh fish on the dock.

After gazing down at the seiners and gillnetters in the harbour, you can learn more of Steveston's fishing and canning history by touring the Gulf of Georgia Cannery, where a 1930s production line clanks through its routine. Finally, if you have not succumbed to Steveston's famous fish and chips, take your picnic lunch to Garry Point Park, sit back and contemplate the ocean or perhaps watch kites being reeled out into the westerly breezes.

Steveston Landing

Finn Slough

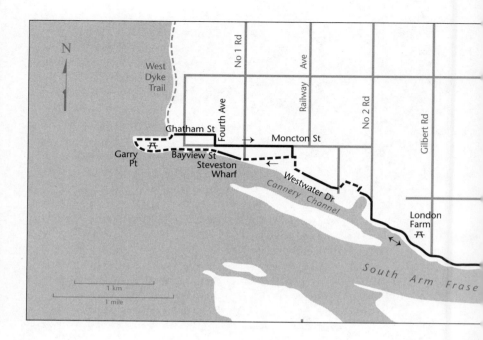

The Route

km 0.0 Horseshoe Slough parking lot. Right (west) on Dyke Road.

1.6 Right on No. 4 Road for a detour through Richmond's fast-disappearing farmland.

2.5 Left on Finn Road.

4.3 Left on No. 3 Road.

5.3 Right on Dyke Road. If you choose to cycle on South Dyke Trail, please be courteous to other users.

6.5 London Farm and Gilbert Beach.

7.2 Follow South Dyke Trail around the marina and along Westwater Drive.

9.0 Left onto gravel track at the sign to Steveston village. This turning is opposite "Britannia at Steveston" condominiums. Follow the wide track as it passes between commercial buildings.

9.7 Left onto Bayview Street. The entrance to the public wharf is on the left. Shops, stalls, restaurants, fish sales on the dock.

Walk west along the wharf toward the harbour and the Gulf of Georgia Cannery. Follow Steveston Greenway signs to Garry Point Park.

10.5 Picnic tables, toilets, Japanese garden, fishermen's memorial, beaches.

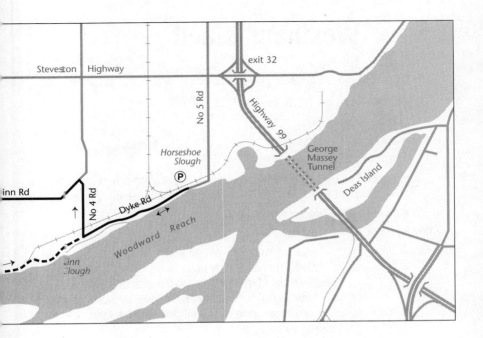

Cycle (slowly) clockwise around Garry Point for a view of the Strait of Georgia and fishboats in Scotch Pond.

Option: Left on West Dyke Trail leads to Terra Nova Park after 5.7 km. Otherwise

11.4 Go east on Chatham Street.

11.8 Right on Fourth Avenue and left on Moncton Street through Steveston village. This stretch is usually busy—walk your bike if you want to look in shop windows.

12.8 Right on footpath at crosswalk opposite Steveston Park then right on road (Britannia condominiums) to pick up the outward route along Westwater Drive and South Dyke Trail.

16.7 Go straight ahead at the gate where No. 3 Road bends left, into the dog off-leash area. Follow the trail around Crown Packaging premises.

18.8 Gate at Finn Slough. Go straight ahead. Buildings on pilings, Dinner Plate Island School, information about Finnish settlement at the bridge.

20.4 Horseshoe Slough parking lot.

9   Westham Island
Delta

Round trip 20.5 km (12 3/4 miles)

Terrain Paved roads; flat

Traffic volume Low, moderate in Ladner

Allow 2 to 2 1/2 hours

Highlights Ladner Harbour Park, George C. Reifel Migratory Bird Sanctuary, berry farms, Canoe Passage, Delta Museum and Archives

Picnic spot Reifel bird sanctuary at 10.1 km

Starting point Ladner Harbour Park

How to get there From Vancouver, turn off Hwy 99 at exit 29 immediately south of the Massey Tunnel. Follow River Road toward Ladner for just over 2 km and turn right across the channel at the sign to Ladner Harbour Park. From other directions, use Ladner Trunk Road (Hwy 10) and turn right on Elliott Street in Ladner and right on River Road.

Although Westham Island could be included in the Ladner Dyke ride, we present it separately because the George C. Reifel Migratory Bird Sanctuary, situated on the estuarine marsh at the mouth of the Fraser River, deserves more than a cursory visit and makes a good family outing.

Outside the entrance is a grassy picnic area, much favoured by panhandling ducks, geese and coots. The refuge is open daily, and for a modest charge you can walk (but not cycle) the 3 kilometres of pathways and visit an interpretive centre in the warming hut. A gift shop is open to all.

Thanks to its protective dykes, Westham Island is rich agricultural land growing corn, potatoes, cabbages and soft fruits. In berry season you might be glad of a spare pannier. All-season cyclists may see flocks of overwintering swans and snow geese feeding in the fields.

The dyke beside River Road West affords glimpses of river traffic, boatyards and floathouse living. If you'd like to see how a local household looked at the turn of the last century, visit the Delta Museum and Archives at Bridge and Delta Streets—the heart of old Ladner.

Delta Museum and Archives

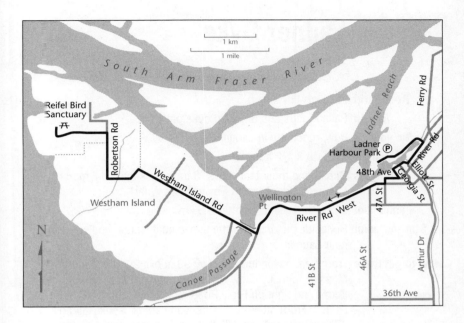

The Route

km **0.0** Ladner Harbour Park. Walking trails, birdwatching. Fishboats and pleasure boats in the channel.

0.5 Right on River Road.

1.0 Right on Elliott Street. An old government wharf lies on the corner of Chisholm Street—fish sales in season. Chisholm becomes Georgia Street.

1.5 Right on 48th Avenue.

1.9 Right on River Road West.

4.2 Wellington Point. View of Canoe Passage and Westham Island.

4.9 Right over Westham Island Road bridge. Caution: this is a single-lane bridge with uneven boards; it is slippery when wet. Westham Island Road becomes Robertson Road.

9.1 Left at sign to George C. Reifel Migratory Bird Sanctuary.

10.1 Parking lot and entrance. Picnic tables, toilets, gift shop.

10.1 Retrace outward route to Westham Island bridge.

15.3 Left on River Road West.

18.4 Left at 47A Street to 48th Avenue.

18.7 Left on Georgia Street, which becomes Chisholm Street.

Option: Go right off Chisholm onto Delta Street to visit Ladner's old town and the Delta Museum. Shops, restaurants, heritage buildings.

Chisholm becomes Elliott Street.

19.6 Left on River Road.

20.0 Left across channel to Ladner Harbour Park.

20.5 Ladner Habour Park parking lot.

10 Ladner Dyke

Delta

Round trip	22.6 km (14 miles)
Terrain	Paved roads and unpaved dyke path; flat
Traffic volume	Low, moderate in Ladner
Allow	2 1/2 to 3 1/2 hours
Highlights	Ocean and mountain views, Canoe Passage, tidal marsh, Ladner's old town and Government Wharf
Picnic spot	Along the dyke path after 9.5 km
Starting point	Roadside parking near the public boat launch on Ferry Road near Ladner
How to get there	From Vancouver, turn off Hwy 99 at exit 29, just south of the Massey Tunnel. Follow River Road toward Ladner for about 2 km, turn right on Ferry Road and continue to the public boat launch. From other directions, use Ladner Trunk Road (Hwy 10) and turn right on Elliott Street in Ladner, right on River Road and left on Ferry Road.

An easy run through the farmland south of Ladner comes to a halt at the causeway leading to Roberts Bank Superport, where long coal trains from the Kootenays and Alberta wait to be unloaded onto freighters bound for Pacific Rim countries.

Beyond the gate onto the dyke, the scene changes. Cycling the countrified dyke between fields and tidal marsh, you share the domain of herons, hawks and waterfowl. In winter, swans and snow geese can often be seen at the water's edge. Take binoculars. In late summer, take a bag for blackberries. Driftwood and sheltering bushes provide a picnic spot below the dyke, with a view across the Strait of Georgia to Vancouver Island. As you round Brunswick Point, look across the cattail marsh for some old pilings—they are the remains of one of the earliest salmon canneries in Delta.

Allow time to explore Ladner's old town around Bridge and Delta Streets; several heritage buildings remain, one of them housing the Delta Museum and Archives. Or pull in at the old government wharf for fresh fish (in season) before you head back to Ferry Road.

Fishboats in Ladner Reach

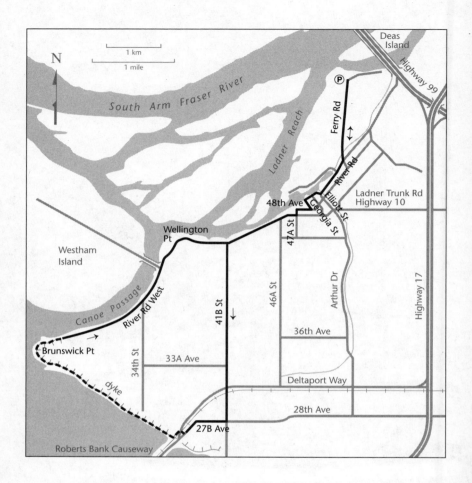

The Route

km 0.0 From roadside parking near the public boat launch, go south on Ferry Road.

1.7 Right on River Road. Ladner Harbour Park is on the right.

2.6 Right on Elliott Street. An old government wharf lies at the corner of Chisholm Street— fish sales in season. Chisholm becomes Georgia Street.

3.1 Right on 48th Avenue.

3.5 Right on River Road West. Floating houses can be seen from the dyke top.

4.9 Left on 41B Street. Expect it to be windy across these open fields.

7.7 Cross Deltaport Way.

8.4 Right on 27B Avenue. Roberts Bank coal port ahead.

9.2 Go right across railway tracks at stop sign just after the bend. Caution: trains are moved electronically, without warning.

Follow dirt track to left.

9.5 Right onto dyke at gate.

Suitable lunch spots can be found near the farm, where paths lead to bushes below the dyke.

12.9 After rounding Brunswick Point you can descend to River Road West at the gate.

16.4 Wellington Point on left. View of Canoe Passage and Westham Island.

18.8 Left at 47A Street to 48th Avenue.

19.1 Left on Georgia Street, which becomes Chisholm Street.

Option: Go right off Chisholm onto Delta Street to visit Ladner's old town and the Delta Museum. Shops, restaurants, heritage buildings.

Chisholm becomes Elliott Street.

20.0 Left on River Road.

20.9 Left on Ferry Road.

22.6 Public boat launch. The road on the right leads to Captain's Cove Marina and Rusty Anchor pub.

11   Boundary Bay

Delta

Round trip 21.2 km (13 1/4 miles)

Terrain Paved roads and gravel dyke; flat

Traffic volume Low, except moderate on Boundary Bay Road

Allow 2 to 3 hours

Highlights Ocean and mountain views; tidal flats and lagoon; raptors, shorebirds, waterfowl; Centennial Beach

Picnic spot Centennial Beach at 10.8 km

Starting point Boundary Bay Airport—roadside parking on approach to the main terminal

How to get there Leave Hwy 99 south of the Massey Tunnel at exit 28. Follow Hwy 17 south for 1.5 km and turn left on Ladner Trunk Road (Hwy 10). Turn right on 80th Street and follow signs to Boundary Bay Airport Main Terminal.

Boundary Bay is of prime importance to migratory and wintering birds hungry for the intertidal plants and animals to be found offshore and in the marsh. Flanking the entire 16-kilometre width of the bay is a gravel dyke, well used by birdwatchers, hikers, joggers and cyclists.

The turnaround point for this ride is Centennial Beach, abutting the U.S. border. Overlooked by Mount Baker on the eastern horizon, you can swim, picnic on the sand or beneath the trees (or at the concession) or explore a self-guided nature trail among the dunes. Please note, though, that cycling is permitted on the multi-use 12th Avenue Dyke Trail only.

Take your binoculars—there are observation towers and viewing platforms along the way.

The Route

km 0.0 Go left (west) from the main terminal approach road.

0.4 Left at the T-junction (72nd Street).

3.0 Right onto the dyke at the end of 72nd Street.

7.1 Right on the footpath where the dyke path ends, and left on Beach Grove Road.

8.4 Cross 12th Avenue and proceed south on Boundary Bay Road.

10.1 Left to Boundary Bay Regional Park (signposted) and follow

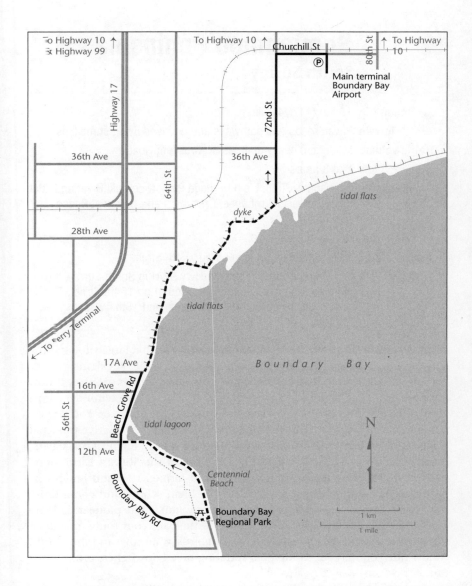

approach road through the parking lot.

10.8 Centennial Beach. Picnic tables, concession (in summer) toilets, trails, swimming.

10.8 Follow the gravel multi-use trail northward. Tidal lagoon and viewing platform.

12.8 At 12th Avenue gate, go right on Beach Grove Road and retrace your outward route via the dyke and 72nd Street.

21.2 Boundary Bay Airport. Skyhawk coffee shop in the main terminal building.

12 Semiahmoo Peninsula
South Surrey

Round trip	18 km (11 1/4 miles)
Terrain	Paved roads and pathways and unpaved dyke; some hills
Traffic volume	Moderate; heavy at times on Crescent Road
Allow	2 to 3 hours
Highlights	Semiahmoo Trail, Elgin Heritage Park, Nicomekl River and tidal flats, Stewart Farmhouse, Crescent Park, Crescent Beach (optional)
Picnic spot	Crescent Park at 10.4 km
Starting point	Bakerview Park parking lot on 154th Street
How to get there	From King George Highway (Hwy 99A) in South Surrey, turn west on 20th Avenue, then left (south) on 154th Street. The park is on the corner of 154th Street and 18th Avenue.

Here's a varied ride around the Semiahmoo Peninsula that largely follows the City of Surrey's designated bike route while avoiding White Rock's major hills.

Once inhabited by Coast Salish people, this sunny corner of Surrey is now a suburban retreat, well served by parks and beaches. Some reminders of its aboriginal and pioneer history have been preserved, however. You'll cycle along a (paved) remnant of the Semiahmoo Trail, an early Native trail that linked tribal villages to the Fraser River fishing grounds. Elgin Heritage Park, on the banks of the Nicomekl River, is the site of the Stewart Farmhouse, built in 1894. The Stewart family dyked and farmed the land beside the Nicomekl River and helped to establish the Elgin school and community hall. Their home is now restored as a living museum where pioneer skills are demonstrated. From the second entrance to the park your route includes a side trip around tidal flats—a haven for songbirds, waterfowl and shorebirds. At low tide you may see sandpipers and long-billed dowitchers probing the mud for worms.

You can take a break in Crescent Park amid beautiful second-growth forest before completing the circuit via pleasant green-belt pathways and along the fringe of Sunnyside Acres Urban Forest.

Stewart Farmhouse, Elgin Heritage Park

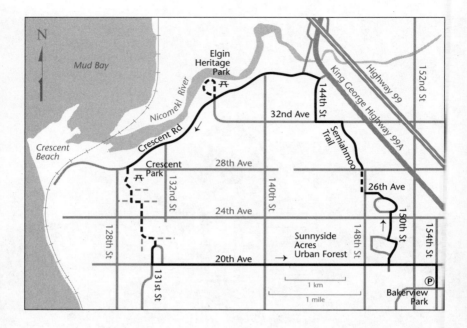

The Route

km **0.0** Left (north) from the Bakerview Park parking lot on 154th Street.

0.4 Left on 20th Avenue.

1.0 Right on 150th Street. Becomes 150A Street.

Left on 22nd Avenue at bend.

1.6 Right on 150th Street.

Cross 24th Avenue and continue on 150th Street, bearing right, downhill.

Left on 25A Avenue on the bend.

2.4 Right on 149th Street. Go downhill.

Left on 26th Avenue on the bend.

2.7 Cross 148th Street and go right on the multi-use pathway.

Left at the top of the overpass.

3.1 Cross 28th Avenue and go left between the posts onto Semiahmoo Trail.

3.8 Small park on right.

4.0 Left on 32nd Avenue, uphill and then down.

4.4 Right on 144th Street. Often busy.

5.2 Left on Crescent Road at the stop sign. Use caution crossing this very busy road.

6.8 Elgin Heritage Park is on the right. Stewart Farmhouse, pole barn, Hooser Weaving Centre, trails, toilets, Nicomekl River.

6.8 Continue on Crescent Road.

7.4 Right at gate to cycle tidal flats loop trail. From the parking lot begin an anticlockwise circuit of the perimeter trail. Nicomekl River, shorebirds and water-fowl, inner marsh.

8.6 Right on Crescent Road after completing tidal flats loop. Hills!

10.4 **Option:** Continue on Crescent Road for a 3-km side trip to Crescent Beach. Seaside village with waterfront path, beach, restaurants. Otherwise

10.4 Left on 129th Street to Crescent Park. Picnic tables, toilets, trails.

10.4 From the park entrance, follow the main multi-use trail, keeping the washroom building on your left. Ignore side trails. Immediately after passing the playground, turn right and continue, keeping the pond on your left. Keep straight ahead at next trail junction. Keep left at the next trail junction and immediately keep left again to skirt the open, grassy area.

11.7 Cross 24th Avenue at the crosswalk and barriers and go straight ahead on paved pathway.

12.0 Take the first path on your left at the end of the curved wooden rail.

12.2 Left at children's slide and benches. The path becomes gravel.

12.5 Right at the open grassy space onto a paved path to the barrier. Right on road (131st Street).

12.9 Left on 20th Avenue.

15.6 Sunnyside Acres Urban Forest. For safety, use the footpath to the top of the hill.

17.7 Right on 154th Street.

18.0 Bakerview Park parking lot.

13 Pitt Polder

Pitt Meadows/Fraser Valley
Regional District

Round trip	31 km (19 1/4 miles)
Terrain	Paved roads and gravel dyke; flat
Traffic volume	Low
Allow	2 1/2 to 3 1/2 hours
Highlights	Pitt Polder, Pitt Lake, mountain views, osprey nests, Alouette River
Picnic spot	Grant Narrows Regional Park at 13.6 km
Starting point	Parking area on Harris Road, south of Alouette River bridge
How to get there	From Lougheed Highway (Hwy 7), turn left on Dewdney Trunk Road just east of Pitt River bridge. Turn left again on Harris Road and drive 2 km to Alouette River bridge.

Nature tamed and untamed could be the theme for this ride. First, the polder: land wrested from the flood plain by human ingenuity. As early as 1911, attempts were made to dyke the area, all ending in flooding or financial disaster. It took Dutch immigrant engineers (and Dutch investment) to overcome the problems. During the 1950s, the first farmsteads were laid out, each with a silo, barn and milking parlour and tenanted by a Dutch farmer.

The marshy northern half of the polder is designated as a Wildlife Management Area and extends to Pitt Lake. From the shores of the 26-kilometre-long lake, the Coast Mountains rise dramatically, often bearing weighty clouds on their shoulders. To the north, from its headwaters on a snowy peak in Garibaldi Park, the upper Pitt River flows through the lake and out again through Grant Narrows, fighting the tides on its way to join the Fraser River.

It is worth cycling out along the Pitt Lake dyke for a view of the lake and the marsh. Keep a lookout for ospreys—their nests have been built on top of the pilings at the edge of the foreshore.

Pitt Lake

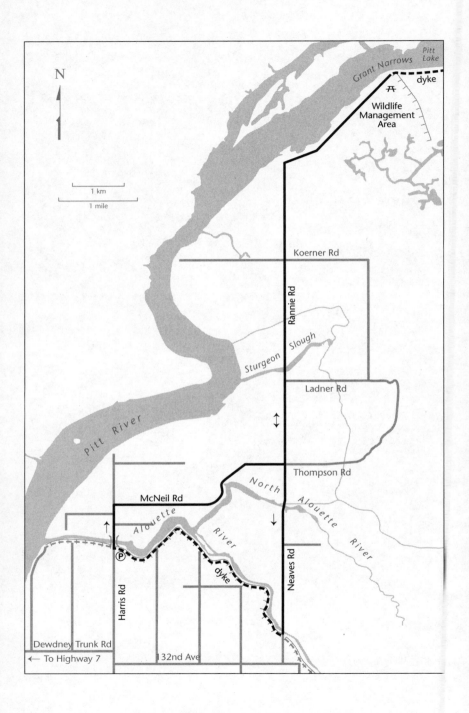

N

1 km
1 mile

Pitt Lake

Grant Narrows

dyke

Wildlife Management Area

Koerner Rd

Rannie Rd

Sturgeon Slough

Ladner Rd

Pitt River

Thompson Rd

North

McNeil Rd

Alouette River

Alouette River

Neaves Rd

P

dyke

Harris Rd

Dewdney Trunk Rd

← To Highway 7

132nd Ave

Sturgeon Slough

The Route

km **0.0** Harris Road parking area. Right (north) on Harris Road and over the bridge.

0.9 Right on McNeil Road. Blueberry farms and tree nurseries.

4.7 Left on Rannie Road.

6.7 Cross Sturgeon Slough. Swaneset Bay Resort is on your left.

13.6 Grant Narrows Regional Park at Pitt Lake. Picnic tables, toilets, concession, canoe rental, walking trails.

Option: Cycle Pitt Lake dyke for wider views. The inner dykes are for walkers only.

13.6 Retrace your outward route on Rannie Road.

22.6 Keep straight ahead where McNeil Road goes right. Rannie Road becomes Neaves Road at this point.

23.4 Cross the North Alouette River and continue on Neaves Road.

26.1 South Alouette River bridge. On the south side of the river, go right onto the dyke path at the gate.

31.0 Harris Road parking area.

14   Pitt Meadows

Pitt Meadows/Maple Ridge

Round trip 29.4 km (18 1/4 miles)

Terrain Paved roads and gravel dyke; a few hills

Traffic volume Low; may be heavy around Port Hammond and Lougheed Highway

Allow 3 to 4 hours

Highlights Pitt and Alouette River dykes, mountain views, quiet country roads, berry farms, waterfowl and songbirds

Picnic spot Benches along the Alouette River dyke after 9.4 km

Starting point Pitt Meadows Civic Centre on Harris Road

How to get there From Lougheed Highway (Hwy 7) east of the Pitt River bridge, turn south on Harris Road and drive about 1 km to the civic centre.

This three-river ramble starts in the urban centre of Pitt Meadows. Incorporated in 1874, the community had its true beginnings in the early 1900s when a dyking system was completed and European immigrants came to build homes and develop farms on the reclaimed land. Dairy farming and berry farming are still the area's main industries.

After exercising your traffic sense and navigational skills through Port Hammond and the outskirts of Haney, you gain the freedom of the dykes. The Alouette River flows from its headwaters on Mt. Robie Reid into Alouette Lake, where it is held captive before being discharged through the dam to wander tamely westward across the plain. From your vantage point on the dyke, you'll see the confluence of the Alouette with the North Alouette, that stream having followed a different course from its birthplace on the Golden Ears massif.

Eventually you arrive, with the Alouette River, at the broad Pitt River. With boats and log booms offshore and blueberry fields on the landward side, you approach the busy Pitt River bridge. That obstacle cleared, 10 kilometres of quiet farm roads take you back to your car.

Alouette reflections

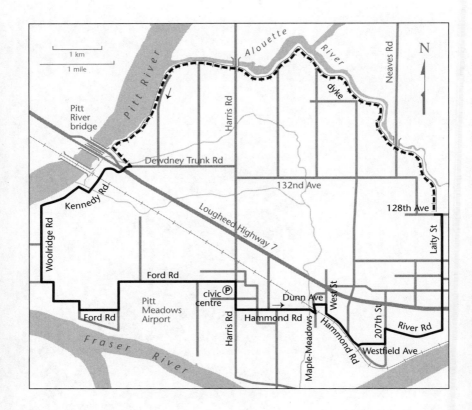

The Route

km 0.0 Pitt Meadows Civic Centre.
Right (south) on Harris Road.

0.5 Left on Hammond Road. Go
downhill.

2.1 Left on Maple-Meadows. Cross
the railway tracks, then turn
immediately right on Dunn
Avenue.

2.4 Right on West Street, which
becomes Hammond Road.

3.7 Left on Westfield Avenue.

4.3 Left on 207th Street.

4.6 Right on River Road.

5.8 Left on Laity Street.

Cross Lougheed Highway and
Dewdney Trunk Road. Busy
intersections.

8.3 Left on 128th Avenue, then
immediately right onto the dyke
path at the gate. Cycle first
beside a ditch, then beside the
Alouette River.

9.4 A pond is on your right. 210th
Street parking area and dyke
access. Continue on the dyke—
benches make good lunch spots.

10.4 Cross Neaves Road and
continue west along the dyke
on the south bank.

Alouette River

13.3 Confluence of Alouette and North Alouette Rivers.

15.3 Enter the parking area. Cross Harris Road and continue west on the dyke on the south bank. There are some low gates on this stretch.

16.7 Alouette River mouth. Continue south beside Pitt River, passing a marina.

19.3 End of dyke at gate. Pitt River bridge lies ahead. Go left on the paved track below the highway, bearing left to join Dewdney Trunk Road at the stop sign.

19.7 Right on Dewdney Trunk Road.

19.8 Cross Lougheed Highway at the traffic light. Caution: very busy intersection.
Keep left and follow Kennedy Road. Note: the dyke path on right becomes rough—the paved roads offer better cycling.

21.8 Left on Woolridge Road.

23.7 Left on Ford Road and follow it through changes of direction. Pitt Meadows Airport is on your right.

29.2 Right on Harris Road.

29.4 Pitt Meadows Civic Centre parking lot is on your right.

15 Golden Ears Park
Maple Ridge

Round trip 24 km (15 miles) or 36 km (22 1/2 miles)

Terrain Paved road, some unpaved road and optional trail; gentle undulations

Traffic volume Low, except moderate on Fern Crescent

Allow 2 to 3 hours, or up to 4 hours for Gold Creek option

Highlights Alouette Lake and beach, coastal forest, views of mountain peaks, Gold Creek (optional), Maple Ridge Park

Picnic spot Alouette Lake day-use area at 12 km

Starting point Maple Ridge Park on 232nd Street

How to get there From the Lougheed Highway (Hwy 7) in Haney, follow Golden Ears Park signs north as far as Maple Ridge Park on the corner of 232nd Street and Fern Crescent.

Few route instructions are needed on this uncomplicated ride into Golden Ears Provincial Park. On Fern Crescent you follow the winding course of the Alouette River, entering the southern end of the park beneath the impassive gaze of a carved wooden mountain goat. Thereafter, you'll notice hiking and equestrian trails leading into the forest on either side.

Many will be content to end the ride with a lazy picnic and swim at Alouette Lake. More energetic cyclists can continue to Gold Creek, where they can follow a short trail to North Beach or take a 2.7-kilometre walk along the creek to Lower Falls. Cycling is not allowed on Lower Falls Trail so pack your bike lock if you intend to include this scenic walk in your itinerary.

Beyond a rugged mountain barrier at its northern end, Golden Ears Park abuts the even larger Garibaldi Provincial Park, making a vast, unbroken stretch of wilderness parkland. The Alouette Valley through which you ride was once the site of B.C.'s largest railway-logging operation. During the 1920s giant firs and cedars fell to the axe and saw—a decade-long harvest that ended when fire swept through the valley in 1931. Cycling between the ranks of today's second-growth forest, you catch glimpses of the ramparts to the west: Alouette Mountain, Evans Peak and the twin peaks of Mount Blanshard known as the Golden Ears.

The Route

km 0.0 Maple Ridge Park parking lot. East on Fern Crescent. This narrow, winding road may be busy at weekends.

4.1 Park entrance. Wooden mountain goat.

12.0 Right to Alouette Lake day-use area. Swimming, long sandy beach, picnic tables, toilets.

Option: Continue on park road for 6 km to Gold Creek day-use area. One-km cycling/hiking trail to North Beach; 2.7-km walking trail to Lower Falls.

12.0 Retrace your outward route to Maple Ridge Park.

24.0 Maple Ridge Park parking lot.

16   Whonnock Lake
Maple Ridge

Round trip	23.5 km (14 1/2 miles)
Terrain	Paved roads and unpaved trail (walk only); several hills, some steep
Traffic volume	Low
Allow	2 1/2 to 3 1/2 hours
Highlights	Quiet, winding roads, woodland trail, side trip to Bell-Irving Fish Hatchery, Kanaka Creek, Whonnock Lake
Picnic spot	Whonnock Lake at 11.5 km
Starting point	Albion Park on 104th Avenue
How to get there	From Lougheed Highway (Hwy 7) east of Haney, turn north on 240th Street, then right on 104th Avenue. The park is on the right after 0.8 km.

On a day when you're feeling energetic and a bit adventurous, you'll enjoy this sporting little ride among the winding lanes near Kanaka Creek.

Maple Ridge abounds in roads that almost but don't quite connect with each other, so your route has many turnings before it reaches Whonnock Lake. To circumvent one of these gaps in the road system, we've directed you along a foot trail through the woods for a short distance. Please walk your bike along this path and be prepared to take a small stream in stride. This digression is far more pleasant than the alternative, which is to cycle 4 kilometres along the Dewdney Trunk Road amid speeding traffic.

A side trip to the Bell-Irving fish hatchery on Kanaka Creek is worthwhile. Free tours are offered most days, on which you may see juvenile salmon and trout in the troughs and rearing ponds. The hatchery releases large numbers of salmon fry into the creek each spring.

After a rest, and perhaps a swim, at Whonnock Lake, you can look forward to plenty of free-wheeling on the homeward lap.

Bell-Irving Hatchery

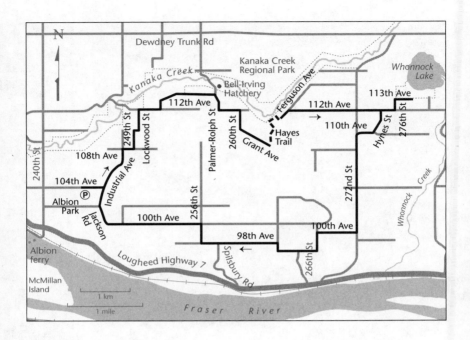

The Route

km 0.0 Albion Park parking lot. East on 104th Avenue.

0.5 Left on Industrial Avenue.

1.5 Right on 108th Avenue.

1.7 Left on 249th Street, which becomes Lockwood Street.

2.6 Right on 112th Avenue.

3.1 Left on 252nd Street, which becomes 112th Avenue.

4.4 Option: For side trip to Bell-Irving hatchery, turn left on 256th Street, then right to the hatchery after 0.2 km. Otherwise

4.4 Right on Palmer-Rolph Street. Left on 112th Avenue.

5.2 Right on 260th Street (signed "No Thru Rd"), which becomes Grant Avenue.

6.3 End of Grant Avenue. Go straight ahead on the signposted Hayes Trail. Please walk bikes on this trail.

Go left at the first trail junction. Cross the bridge over the creek and keep left. Cross the second creek—there may be a plank bridge.

7.8 Right onto a wide equestrian trail that emerges on Ferguson Avenue.

8.1 Right on 112th Avenue.

Canada Goose

10.£ Left on 276th Street at the sign to Whonnock Lake, and follow the road to the main parking lot near the beach.

11.£ Beach parking. Picnic tables, toilets, swimming.

11.£ Retrace your route to 112th Avenue.

12.£ Right on 112th Avenue.

12.£ Left on Hynes Street.

13.£ Right on 110th Avenue.

13.6 Left on 272nd Street. Narrow shoulder—use caution.

15.8 Right on 100th Avenue. Sudden steep hill—find a low gear quickly!

16.6 Left on 268th Street. Steep downhill.

Right on 98th Avenue.

17.8 Jog right on 264th Street.

18.0 Left on 98th Avenue.

19.6 Right on 256th Street.

20.0 Left on 100th Avenue.

Bear right on Jackson Road.

22.4 Right on Industrial Avenue.

22.8 Left on 104th Avenue.

23.3 Albion Park parking lot.

17 Stave Dams

Mission

Round trip	26 km (16 1/4 miles)
Terrain	Paved roads; rolling hills, some steep
Traffic volume	Low to moderate
Allow	2 1/2 to 4 hours
Highlights	Stave and Ruskin Dams, Hayward Lake, side trip to Rolley Lake Provincial Park, Stave River
Picnic spot	Mill Pond on Dewdney Trunk Road at 10.8 km or Hayward Lake Recreation Area at 18.6 km
Starting point	Ruskin Recreation Site on Hayward Street east of Ruskin Dam
How to get there	Follow Lougheed Highway (Hwy 7) east from Maple Ridge towards Mission and turn left on 287th Street. After about 3 km turn right to cross Ruskin Dam and continue for less than 1 km to signposted Ruskin Recreation Site.

Although fairly challenging, this circuit around the Stave Dams near Mission is not beyond the ability of an "easy" cyclist equipped with low gears, good brakes and a bit of courage. The landscape is majestic, whether viewed from the dam walls or from the rolling hills of historic Dewdney Trunk Road— originally an overland coach route from Dewdney to Port Moody.

The generation of hydroelectric power from Alouette and Stave Lakes began in the early 1900s. Before the construction of the Stave and Ruskin Dams, the Stave River flowed unchecked through a forested valley. Today, it passes through the Stave Falls powerhouse (currently undergoing redevelopment) into Hayward Lake Reservoir before being released from the Ruskin powerhouse to flow into the Fraser River.

Optional side trips to Rolley Lake Provincial Park and Hayward Lake Recreation Site reward the energetic. Others may be content to walk down to the spawning channels at Ruskin Recreation Site for a close-up view of the Stave River unleashed.

The Route

km 0.0 Ruskin Recreation Site. Right (east) onto Hayward Street.

1.1 Left on Keystone Avenue. A steep uphill for 1.2 km, then a more gradual ascent.

7.4 Left on Dewdney Trunk Road. Uphill again.

10.8 Mill Pond is on your right. This is a well-deserved rest or picnic spot on the rocks beside the water.

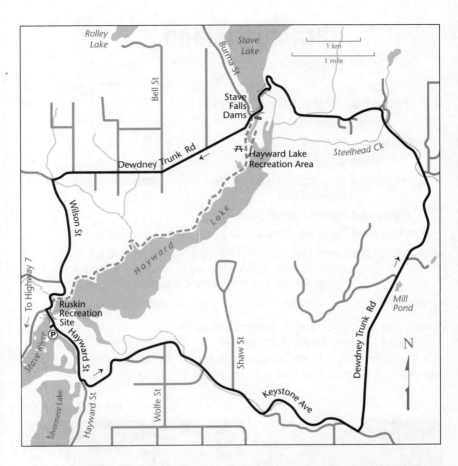

10.8 Continue on Dewdney Trunk
Road. You follow gentle rolling
hills through Steelhead, then
make a steep, winding descent
to the Stave Dams.

17.8 Cross the Stave Falls Dams.
Watch for oncoming traffic and
beware of the railway track in
the roadbed.

18.6 Option: Left goes to Hayward
Lake Recreation Area. Picnic
tables, toilets, beach, trails.
Add 1 km for this side trip.
Otherwise continue west on
Dewdney Trunk Road.

20.9 Option: Right on Bell Street
leads to Rolley Lake Provincial
Park. Picnic area, beach, trails,
interpretive centre. Add 7 km
for this side trip. Otherwise
continue west on Dewdney
Trunk Road.

22.5 Left on Wilson Street. Steep
winding descent.

25.5 Left across Ruskin Dam.

26.0 Right to Ruskin Recreation Site.
Picnic tables, toilets, path to
spawning channels and Stave
River.

18   Barnston Island
Langley

Round trip 10 km (6 1/4 miles) or more
Terrain Paved road; flat
Traffic volume Very low
Allow 1 to 1 1/2 hours
Highlights Ferry crossing, farms, river and mountain views, Robert Point Regional Park
Picnic spot Robert Point at 8.9 km
Starting point Ferry slip at the end of 104th Avenue (Hjorth Road)
How to get there Leave Hwy 1, east of the Port Mann bridge, at exit 53 and drive north on 176th Street. After about 1.5 km, turn right on 104th Avenue and proceed to the parking lot at the ferry slip.

Sometimes you want a safe, undemanding ride that even little legs and wheels can manage. Barnston Island, lying in the Fraser River's Surrey Bend, is a favourite with cycling families. Leave your car at the slip; a free ferry ride—sound your horn to summon the boat—is part of the fun.

Leaving Robert Point

The paved road you cycle on is the top of a dyke encircling the entire island. The inland landscape is a patchwork of fields, while the river beyond the dyke provides a changing scene. In Parsons Channel, fishboats, barges and float planes go about their business to the music of a nearby sawmill. After rounding Mann Point at the island's eastern end, you enter Bishops Reach. Paths lead down to the river, where you can look across the log booms to Pitt Meadows airport on the opposite shore.

All too soon, you reach Robert Point at the northwest tip of the island. Follow the loop trail to the beach and picnic site. A short homestretch, enhanced by a view of Mount Baker, brings you back to the ferry stage. Not long enough? Go round again.

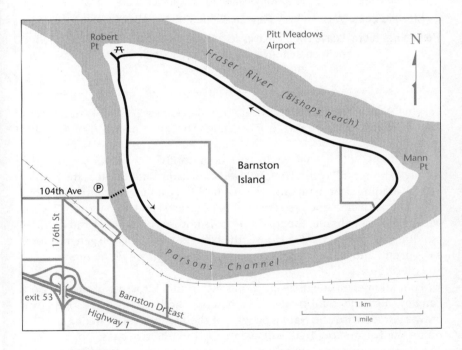

The Route

km **0.0** Disembark from the ferry and begin an anticlockwise circuit. River traffic in Parsons Channel.

4.3 Mann Point. Wild roses in the summer. View upstream to Golden Ears.

8.9 Robert Point Regional Park with picnic tables, toilets. View downstream toward Port Mann bridge.

10.0 Ferry slip.

19   Fort Langley
Langley

Round trip	24.5 km (15 1/4 miles)
Terrain	Paved roads and optional unpaved trail; rolling hills
Traffic volume	Low to moderate
Allow	2 1/2 to 3 1/2 hours
Highlights	Telegraph Trail, Fort Langley, Fraser River views, historic site, Fort-to-Fort Trail, Edgewater Bar
Picnic spot	Fort Langley National Historic Site picnic area at 12.1 km
Starting point	West Langley Park on 208th Street in Walnut Grove
How to get there	Leave Hwy 1 at exit 58 and drive north on 200th Street. Turn right on 96th Avenue and right on 208th Street. The park is on the left after 0.5 km.

Leaving Walnut Grove, a long and glorious descent on Telegraph Trail speeds you on your way. Thereafter, there is much to stop and look at on this historical ride.

Entering Fort Langley from its back door on River Road, you glimpse the restored Hudson's Bay fort from below its stockade. Built on this site in 1839 as a fur-trading post, Fort Langley became a large and busy centre, employing an army of craftsmen to serve trappers, farmers and gold miners. Today, within the log palisade, the fort comprises both reconstructed and original buildings, including the Big House (the officers' quarters), the general store, a cooperage and a blacksmith's forge. Costumed staff are on hand to answer any questions.

Four kilometres downstream, along your route, is the site of the first Fort Langley, hurriedly built in 1827 as a base for the Hudson's Bay Company's growing trade with the Native peoples of the Fraser River. A hiking/cycling route, the Fort-to-Fort Trail, will eventually link the two sites. Opposite the commemorative cairn is a restored 1909 homestead as well as access to the Houston Trail (for walkers only) through the forest.

Finally, turn in at the entrance to Derby Reach Regional Park, 2 kilometres ahead, to visit Edgewater Bar before heading home.

Fort-to-Fort Trail

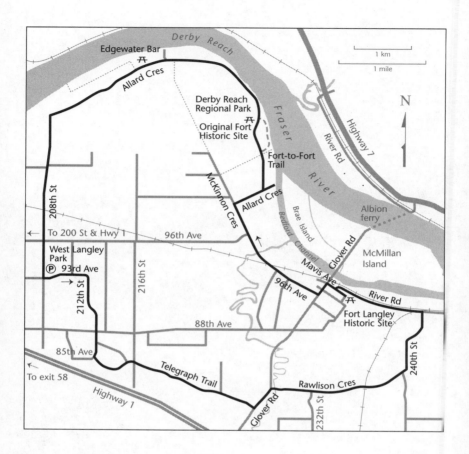

The Route

km **0.0** West Langley Park parking lot. Left on 208th Street.

0.3 Left on 93rd Avenue.

1.1 Right on 212th Street.

Cross 88th Avenue at the traffic lights. Busy intersection.

2.7 Left on Telegraph Trail.

Cross 216th Street and begin a long downhill with views.

5.9 Left on Glover Road. Use caution at this junction.

6.3 Right on Rawlison Crescent.

7.0 Stay left on Rawlison where 232nd Street joins.

8.0 Railway tunnel. Go uphill shortly after.

8.8 Keep left at junction onto 240th Street (may not be signposted at this point).

10.1 Left on River Road.

11.9 Left on Mavis Avenue.

12.1 Fort Langley National Historic Site. Museums, picnic tables, toilets.

12.4 From Mavis Avenue turn left on Glover Road. Shops and restaurants in Fort Langley village.

12.7 Right on 96th Avenue. Use the sidewalk where the road narrows at the bridge.

14.4 Keep straight ahead on McKinnon Crescent where 96th Avenue bears left. Pass Fort Langley Golf Course.

15.1 Right on Allard Crescent.

16.4 Option: Fort-to-Fort Trail, signposted on right, leads to a heritage area. Otherwise continue along the road, past the beaver pond, to the same point.

17.1 Cairn marking the site of the original fort, Fraser River, Houston House (not open to the public) and restored farm buildings opposite. Picnic tables, toilets.

Option: A walking/cycling path running parallel to the road leads to Derby Reach Regional Park. Otherwise continue on Allard Crescent.

19.2 Park entrance to Edgewater Bar. Picnic tables, toilets, camping, fishing.

Continue on Allard Crescent past fields dyked for cranberry bogs.

21.5 Left on 208th Street. Cross the railway, then 96th Avenue.

24.5 Left into West Langley Park parking lot.

Site of first Fort Langley

20 Glen Valley
Langley/Abbotsford

Round trip	33.4 km (20 3/4 miles) or 39.7 km (24 1/2 miles)
Terrain	Paved roads; some flat, some hills; several railway crossings
Traffic volume	Low, except around Fort Langley
Allow	3 1/2 to 4 1/2 hours
Highlights	Fort Langley village and museums, Telegraph Trail, Fraser River, Glen Valley Regional Park
Picnic spot	Poplar Bar at 22.8 km
Starting point	Fort Langley National Historic Park
How to get there	Leave Hwy 1 at exit 58 or 66 to Fort Langley.

This route along the gentle hills east of Langley takes you through rolling farmland and tucked-away neighbourhoods before descending to the scenic Fraser River.

From the first rise, on 240th Street, the sight of zebras and ostriches in the fields of a game farm affords the perfect excuse to dismount. Next comes a peaceful interlude along a section of historic Telegraph Trail, once part of an overland telegraph route begun in 1865 to link Russia to the United States— a project doomed by the laying of a communications cable beneath the Atlantic Ocean the following year.

After a steep, winding descent to the floor of the valley you'll see land being used for cranberry production. This is not as innovative as you might think: during the 1850s cranberries harvested by aboriginal peoples were packed at Fort Langley to be sent to San Francisco.

Glen Valley Regional Park includes Duncan, Poplar and Two-Bit Bars. At Poplar Bar, our suggested picnic spot, you can rest or enjoy your lunch on the riverbank. Opposite is Crescent Island. The Fraser sweeps around it, bearing tugs, fishboats and debris; geese and goldeneye brave the current. Amid the turbid water, millions of migrating salmon travel up or downstream according to their season. Two-Bit Bar, reached at 24.7 kilometres, is notable for Hassall House, dating back to 1917. The house stands on rental property and is not open to the public.

Whether you cycle the entire route or choose the shorter option, take time to browse among Fort Langley's tea rooms, craft shops and antiques stores or visit the restored Hudson's Bay Company fort and adjacent museums.

Stopping to smell the roses

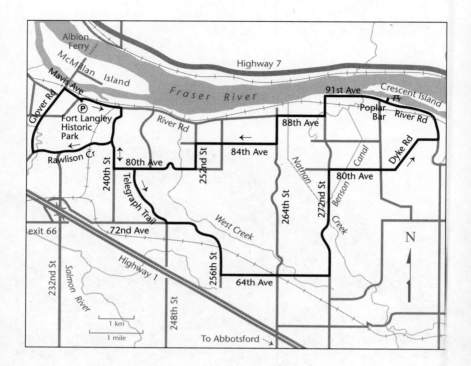

The Route

km **0.0** Fort Langley National Historic Park parking lot on Mavis Avenue.

0.2 Right on River Road.

1.8 Right on 240th Street.

3.2 Stay left on 240th Street at the junction with Rawlison Crescent. The game farm is on the right near the top of the hill.

4.1 Left on 80th Avenue.

4.7 Right on Telegraph Trail. Historic route.

6.8 Left on 72nd Avenue, which becomes 72nd Diversion.

8.6 Right on 256th Street.

9.7 Left on 64th Avenue.

11.4 Cross 264th Street at the stop sign.

13.0 Left on 272nd Street. Steep, winding descent—try not to fly past your next turning!

16.5 Right on 80th Avenue, which becomes Marsh-McCormick Road. Cranberry bogs.

Cross Lefeuvre Road.

18.6 Left on Dyke Road, which becomes Gray Avenue.

20.2 Left on Bradner Road.

21.0 Left on River Road. Optional hiking/cycling path along the riverbank leads to Poplar Bar.

22.8 Right at the gate to Poplar Bar, Glen Valley Regional Park.

Llama stepping out

Picnic tables, toilets, information kiosk.

22.8 Continue west on River Road, which becomes 91st Avenue.

24.7 Two-Bit Bar is on the bend. Historic building.

25.4 Right on 88th Avenue.

26.9 **Option:** The route described includes a very steep hill and a busy stretch of Glover Road. For a shorter (6.5 km) and flatter route to Fort Langley, continue on 88th Avenue and River Road. Otherwise go left on 264th Street.

27.7 Right on 84th Avenue.

30.1 Left on 252nd Street.

31.9 Right on 80th Avenue. Steep hill—be prepared to push your bicycle.

33.7 Right on 240th Street.

34.6 Left on Rawlison Crescent. Use caution at this junction.

36.3 Keep right at junction with 232nd Street.

37.0 Right on Glover Road. Traffic may be heavy.

39.0 Fort Langley village.

Right on Mavis Avenue.

39.7 Fort Langley National Historic Park parking lot.

21 Campbell River Valley
Langley

Round trip	23.6 km (14 3/4 miles)
Terrain	Paved roads; rolling hills
Traffic volume	Low to moderate; may be busy on 16th Avenue
Allow	2 1/2 to 3 1/2 hours
Highlights	Country roads among farms and stables; Campbell Valley Regional Park: visitor centre, Annand/Rowlatt farmhouse, Lochiel schoolhouse, wildlife garden; Noel Booth Park
Picnic spot	Campbell Valley Regional Park (south entrance) at 13.8 km
Starting point	Roadside parking at Noel Booth Community Park on 36th Avenue
How to get there	From Fraser Highway (Hwy 1A) or Hwy 1 exit 58, drive south on 200th Street. Turn left (east) on 36th Avenue.

Ever seeking quiet roads, our route jogs southward in easy stages, taking you through quiet residential neighbourhoods, past eclectic hobby farms and horse paddocks.

Here and there among Langley's gentle hills stand old barns, split-rail fences and skeletal remnants of orchards—memorials to the region's pioneer farmers. One of the earliest settlers in this valley was Alexander Annand, whose restored 1898 homestead stands in Campbell Valley Regional Park. Nearby, the one-room Lochiel schoolhouse has come to rest in the park after having been moved three times and having done duty as a community hall.

The park's uplands and wetlands surrounding the Campbell River provide habitat for many varied animals, birds and plants. Cycling is not permitted in the park, but nature lovers can lock their bikes to the cycle rack and explore on foot. The Campbell River (more correctly, the Little Campbell River) takes a northward swing through the valley, thereby crossing your path once again before resuming its westward journey to Semiahmoo Bay.

Old barn near Langley

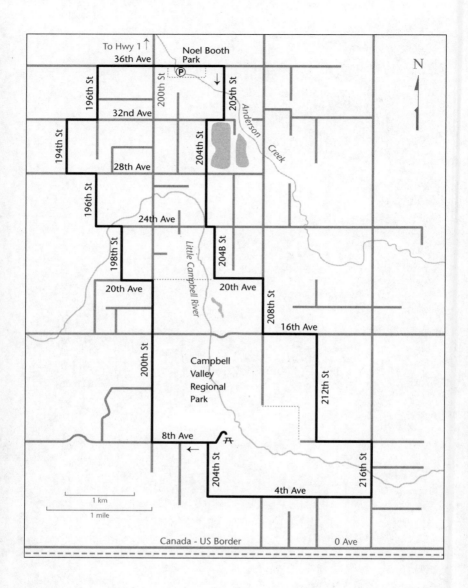

To Hwy 1 ↑
Noel Booth Park
36th Ave
Ⓟ
196th St
200th St
205th St
N
32nd Ave
194th St
Anderson Creek
196th St
204th St
28th Ave
24th Ave
Little Campbell River
198th St
204B St
20th Ave
20th Ave
208th St
16th Ave
200th St
Campbell Valley Regional Park
212th St
8th Ave
216th St
204th St
1 km
4th Ave
1 mile
Canada - US Border
0 Ave

The Route

km **0.0** Noel Booth Community Park. East on 36th Avenue.

0.8 Right on 205th Street.

1.6 Right on 32nd Avenue.

1.8 Left on 204th Street. Lakes are visible on the left.

3.4 Jog left on 24th Avenue.

3.6 Right on 204B Street.

Left on 20th Avenue.

5.1 Right on 208th Street.

5.9 Left on 16th Avenue. Busy main road.

6.7 Right on 212th Street. Go uphill, then down a longer hill.

8.4 Left on 8th Avenue.

9.2 Right on 216th Street. Cross Campbell River.

10.0 Right on 4th Avenue. Go gradually uphill.

Right on 204th Street.

Left on 8th Avenue.

13.4 Right to Campbell Valley Regional Park. Follow the driveway to the second parking lot.

13.8 Information kiosk; picnic tables to right, past washroom building; visitor centre; wildlife garden; walking trails. Cycling is not permitted in the park.

13.8 Continue west on 8th Avenue.

15.0 Right on 200th Street, which may be busy north of 16th Avenue.

17.5 Left on 20th Avenue.

17.9 Right on 198th Street.

18.7 Left on 24th Avenue. Cross Campbell River.

19.1 Right on 196th Street.

19.9 Left on 28th Avenue.

20.4 Right on 194th Street.

21.2 Right on 32nd Avenue.

21.6 Left on 196th Street.

22.4 Right on 36th Avenue.

23.6 Noel Booth Community Park. Paths, lake, picnic tables.

22   Aldergrove
Langley/Abbotsford

Round trip 25.7 km (16 miles)

Terrain Paved roads and unpaved cycle path; some flat, some rolling hills

Traffic volume Moderate; heavy around Aldergrove and on Lefeuvre Road

Allow 2 1/2 to 3 1/2 hours

Highlights Roadside berry stalls in season, Aldergrove Lake Regional Park, views of Mount Baker and the Golden Ears

Picnic spot Aldergrove Lake Regional Park at 16.6 km

Starting point Aldergrove City Park on 32nd Avenue

How to get there From Fraser Highway (Hwy 1A), turn north on Hwy 13 (264th Street), then immediately right on 32nd Avenue. Enter the park after 1.5 km, immediately after passing the sports field.

Aldergrove, known for tasty German sausages, also boasts a telephone museum and one of the oldest agricultural fairs in B.C. Leaving the small city park you bowl along the hills and dales of southeast Langley, passing tree nurseries and berry farms interspersed with paddocks and stables—evidence of Langley Township's claim to be "The Horse Capital of B.C."

A short stretch along the 49th parallel brings you to Aldergrove Lake Regional Park, whose man-made lake is enormously popular on summer weekends. This area is rich in gravel deposits left by retreating glaciers; the park's lake and ponds have been created from reclaimed gravel pits—work that is still going on.

Much of the park is wooded and crisscrossed with a network of walking and equestrian trails, some of which are open to cyclists as a pilot project (consult a park leaflet). For anywhere other than the short cycle trail around the lake, you will need a mountain bike and plenty of energy. The ride back to Aldergrove may be enough. In berry season you can fill up an empty pannier from roadside stalls along the way.

Borderline refreshments

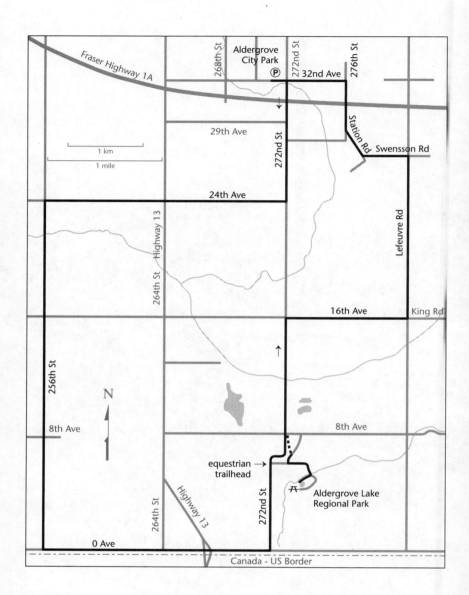

The Route

km 0.0 Aldergrove City Park parking lot. Left (east) on 32nd Avenue. The telephone museum is on the corner of 32nd Avenue and 271st Street.

0.2 Right on 272nd Street.

1.9 Right on 24th Avenue.

5.2 Left on 256th Street. Undulating road. Pass several stables.

10.0 Left on 0 Avenue. This road runs along the Canada/U.S. border. There are raspberry farms and nurseries on your left.

12.2 Cross Hwy 13 north of the border crossing and continue on 0 Avenue. Boundary Road in the U.S. runs parallel on your right.

13.3 Left on 272nd Street. Your climb is gradual, becoming steeper after the bend. Pass Equestrian Trailhead.

15.5 At the corner of 272nd Street and 8th Avenue a signposted cycling trail enters Aldergrove Lake Regional Park, joining the paved access road at an information kiosk. Continue right on the access road, pass a sheltered picnic area in the field and turn right after the bridge.

16.6 The main parking lot is near the lake. Picnic tables, bike rack, toilets, trails.

16.6 Return to 8th Avenue and 272nd Street via the road and the cycling trail.

17.7 North on 272nd Street. Berry farms.

19.3 Right on 16th Avenue, which becomes King Road. Be prepared for gravel trucks on weekdays.

20.9 Left on Lefeuvre Road.

23.1 Left on Swensson Road.

23.7 Right on Station Road.

24.1 Bear right on 276th Street and cross Fraser Highway (Hwy 1A) at the traffic light.

24.8 Left on 32nd Avenue.

25.7 Aldergrove City Park parking lot.

Telephone Museum

Miracle Valley

Fraser Valley Regional District

Round trip	25.4 km (15 3/4 miles)
Terrain	Paved roads and short unpaved trail; some hills
Traffic volume	Low, possibly moderate on Sylvester Road
Allow	2 1/2 to 3 1/2 hours
Highlights	Farmlands and mountain views, Allen Lake, Cascade Creek and waterfall, Davis Lake Provincial Park (optional)
Picnic spot	Cascade Falls Regional Park at 11.4 km
Starting point	Hatzic Prairie Community Hall on Farms Road
How to get there	From Lougheed Highway (Hwy 7) about 6.5 km east of Mission, turn left on Sylvester Road, then left on Farms Road. The community hall is at the junction of Farms and Dale Road.

Extending northward from Hatzic Lake is a narrow valley crisscrossed by numerous creeks born in the mountain ramparts to the east. The route described takes you from the gentle farmlands of Hatzic Prairie to the sterner region through which Cascade Creek makes its helter-skelter descent. From our suggested picnic spot beside the creek, a foot trail climbs 90 metres to the spectacular double falls—an approach that is more in keeping with the spirit of the cascades than the gravel vehicle road.

On your return route to the prairie, Stave Lake Road provides a pleasing descent before passing through a quaintly rustic neighbourhood tucked against the western hillside. Rock climbers are often seen tackling the bluffs along here.

Be warned that a sudden thunderstorm in the Hatzic area is not uncommon and while you may enjoy the sight and sound as it rolls around the surrounding mountains, you'd be wise to keep rain gear handy on this outing.

Hatzic Prairie Market

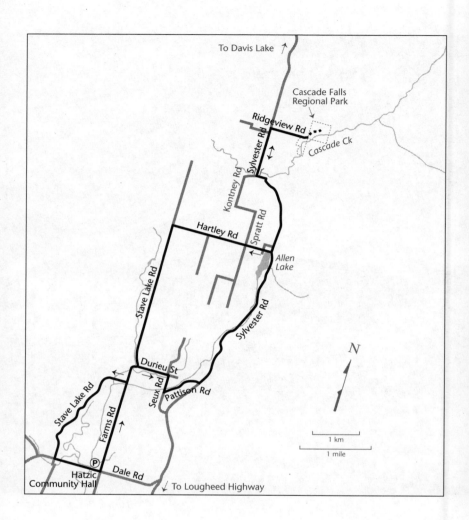

To Davis Lake

Cascade Falls
Regional Park

Ridgeview Rd

Sylvester Rd

Kontney Rd

Cascade Ck

Hartley Rd

Spratt Rd

Allen
Lake

Stave Lake Rd

Sylvester Rd

N

Durieu St

Seux Rd

Pattison Rd

Stave Lake Rd

Farms Rd

1 km

1 mile

P

Hatzic
Community Hall

Dale Rd

To Lougheed Highway

The Route

km 0.0 Hatzic Prairie Community Hall parking lot. Left (north) on Farms Road.

2.5 Straight ahead on Durieu Street after bend.

3.2 Right on Seux Road. Straight ahead is "No Thru Road."

3.6 Left on Pattison Road.

4.6 Left on Sylvester Road. This is a narrow, winding road with ups and downs.

Pass Allen Lake on your left. No public access to water.

10.2 Cross the bridge over Cascade Creek.

10.6 Ridgeview Road and sign "Cascade Falls Regional Park."

Option: 3.5 km ahead on Sylvester Road is Davis Lake Provincial Park as an alternative destination—some hills on the way. Otherwise, go right on Ridgeview Road.

11.4 Gate. The gravel vehicle road continues to the top of the falls but a gated track on the right leads to a picnic spot beside the creek, from which the cascades can be reached by a foot trail.

11.4 Return on Ridgeview Road.

12.2 Left on Sylvester Road.

15.3 Right on Hartley Road. Steep hill.

17.6 Left on Stave Lake Road. Ups and downs.

20.9 Keep right on Stave Lake Road at the bend where Durieu Street goes left.

21.4 Right to stay on Stave Lake Road. Watch closely for this turning, which is immediately before the bridge. Narrow, winding road.

24.2 Left on Dale Road.

25.4 Hatzic Prairie Community Hall at the junction with Farms Road. Refreshments available at Hatzic Prairie Market opposite.

24 Nicomen Island
Fraser River Regional District

Round trip	22 km (13 3/4 miles)
Terrain	Paved roads and gravel road; flat
Traffic volume	Low, except for a short stretch of Lougheed Highway
Allow	1 1/2 to 2 1/2 hours
Highlights	Quiet country roads, waterfowl in Nicomen Slough, Quaamitch Slough, old store in Deroche
Starting point	On North Nicomen Road in Deroche. Park beside the railway tracks opposite Deroche Community Hall.
How to get there	Drive east from Mission on Lougheed Highway (Hwy 7) about 21 km to Deroche. Turn left onto North Nicomen Road immediately after the bridge.

Nicomen Island is the largest of several islands encompassed by the Fraser River and Nicomen Slough. Despite being bisected by the Lougheed Highway, the island remains a sleepy backwater where the cyclist can pedal beside the wide, slow-moving slough and among the thriving farms. A dyke protects the island from encroachment by the Fraser River, but as its path is fairly rough and gated at frequent intervals, the winding Nicomen Island Trunk Road affords a more comfortable ride.

We have not yet found the perfect picnic spot on Nicomen Island; instead, we reload our bikes and drive 15 kilometres east on Lougheed Highway (Hwy 7) to Kilby Provincial Park on Harrison Bay. Here, there are picnic tables behind the Kilby General Store Museum or a homestyle lunch in the Harrison River Tea Room. Kilby is not large enough for a grand tour, but you can cycle to the end of Kilby Road and back, or through the tiny settlement to the bay, where the Harrison River gathers itself before entering the narrow channel to the Fraser.

An alternative to the lazy outing described is to combine the Nicomen Island route with the Dewdney dyke. For this you must brave the Lougheed Highway west of the Nicomen Island Trunk Road turnaround point, cross the bridge over Nicomen Slough and immediately turn left onto River Road South. From there, a further 9 kilometres of dyke and farm roads are yours to explore.

Nicomen Slough

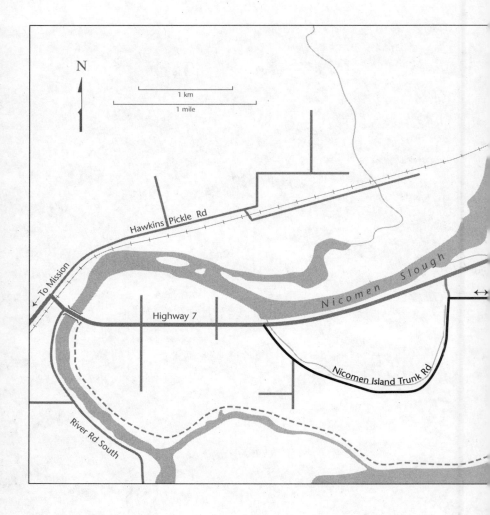

The Route

km **0.0** Deroche Community Hall. Right onto Lougheed Highway and cross the bridge over Nicomen Slough. Continue west on the highway; for a better view of the slough you can cycle on the dyke top, but return to the pavement before reaching the gate to private property.

3.5 Right on Ross Road, which becomes Nicomen Island Slough Road at the bend.

6.0 Left on Johnson Road.

Cross Lougheed Highway.

8.1 Right on Nicomen Island Trunk Road.

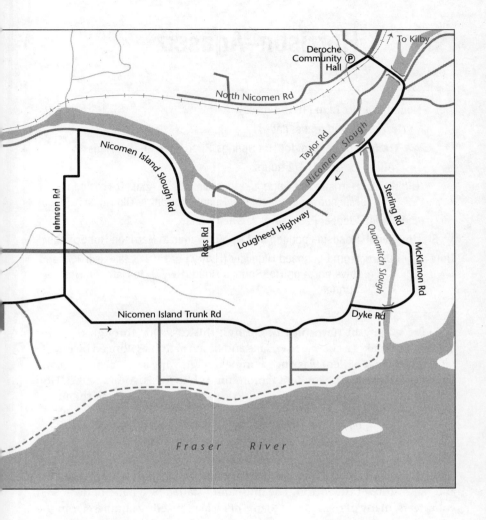

11.1 Turnaround point at the junction with Lougheed Highway. Retrace your route on Nicomen Island Trunk Road to avoid using the busy highway.

14.1 Johnson Road on left. Stay right to continue east on Nicomen Island Trunk Road.

19.2 Right on Dyke Road. Cross Quaamitch Slough.

19.9 Left on McKinnon Road, which becomes Sterling Road.

21.7 Right on Lougheed Highway. Left on North Nicomen Road after the bridge.

22.0 Deroche Community Hall.

25   Harrison–Agassiz
Kent

Round trip	30.1 km (18 3/4 miles)
Terrain	Paved roads; flat
Traffic	Low, except for Hot Springs Road (Hwy 9) and Agassiz
Allow	2 1/2 to 3 1/2 hours
Highlights	Harrison Hot Springs, mountain views, Agassiz-Harrison Museum and Agricultural Research Centre, Old Agassiz Place
Picnic spot	Pioneer Park in Agassiz at 18.2 km
Starting point	Roadside parking on Lillooet Avenue in Harrison Hot Springs
How to get there	From Lougheed Highway (Hwy 7) or Hwy 1, take exit 135 and drive north on Hot Springs Road (Hwy 9) to Harrison Hot Springs.

If you're staying in Harrison Hot Springs, this easy ride through the Kent countryside makes a change from lake and beach activities. Ringed by mountains, the district of Kent was once a prime hop-growing area, taking its name from the English county of Kent famous for its hop fields. After the B.C. Hop Company moved to Creston in 1952, corn and dairying became the mainstay of Kent's economy.

After a rest in Pioneer Park and a saunter through the town, do allow time to visit the Agassiz-Harrison Museum. Housed in the 1893 Canadian Pacific railway station, complete with caboose and relocated to the grounds of the Agricultural Research Centre, artifacts and displays depict both the pioneer and rail history of the region. The museum is staffed by a band of dedicated volunteers, many of them descendants of local pioneering families. From the story of its earliest settlers, Thomas B. Hicks and Captain Lewis Agassiz, and the doings of Dr. McCaffrey (who tended his practice by riding the rails on a hand-propelled speeder) to an account of the 1948 Fraser Valley flood when water surged through the town, Kent's lively history is lovingly preserved.

Agassiz barn

Watching the world go by

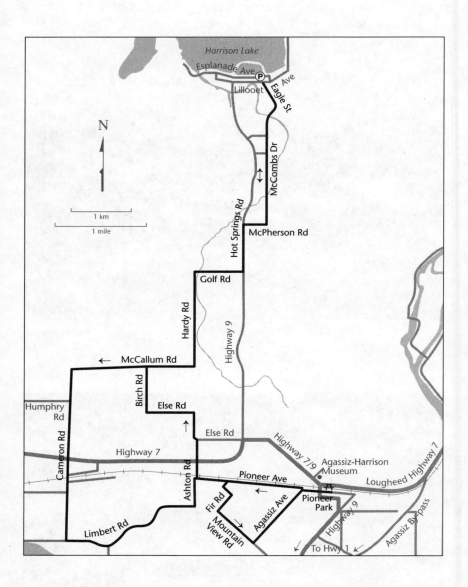

N

1 km
1 mile

Harrison Lake

Esplanade Ave

Lillooet

Eagle St

Eagle Ave

McCombs Dr

Hot Springs Rd

McPherson Rd

Golf Rd

Hardy Rd

Highway 9

McCallum Rd

Birch Rd

Else Rd

Humphry Rd

Cameron Rd

Else Rd

Highway 7

Ashton Rd

Fir Rd

Mountain View Rd

Pioneer Ave

Agassiz Ave

Highway 7/9

Agassiz-Harrison Museum

Pioneer Park

Lougheed Highway 7

Highway 9

Agassiz Bypass

Limbert Rd

To Hwy 1

The Route

km **0.0** From Lillooet Avenue go right (south) on Eagle Street.

0.8 Cross Miami River. Eagle Street becomes McCombs Drive.

2.6 Right on McPherson Road.

2.9 Left on Hot Springs Road (Hwy 9).

3.8 Right on Golf Road, which becomes Hardy Road.

6.3 Right on McCallum Road, which becomes Cameron Road.

8.9 Cross Lougheed Highway (Hwy 7) and the railway tracks.

11.4 Left on Limbert Road. The road curves around the base of Cemetery Hill.

13.4 The old cemetery lies on your left.

Limbert Road becomes Ashton Road.

14.4 Straight ahead on Pioneer Avenue where Ashton Road crosses the railway.

15.0 Right on Fir Road. There is an alpaca ranch at the bend. Hopyard Hill lies on your right.

Fir Road becomes Mountain View Road, with a view of Mount Cheam and its surrounding peaks.

16.5 Left on Agassiz Avenue. Built in 1867, the old Agassiz Place on your right was the home of the Agassiz family. The house is now a private residence.

17.7 Right on Pioneer Avenue. Pass Agassiz Fairgrounds.

18.2 Pioneer Park is on your left. Picnic tables. The Aberdeen Visitor Centre is adjacent.

18.2 Return west on Pioneer Avenue. For a side trip to the Agassiz-Harrison Museum, turn right (north) on Hwy 7/9 and follow the sign to the museum after 0.3 km. Otherwise continue on Pioneer Avenue.

20.7 Right on Ashton Road and cross the railway tracks.

21.3 Left on Else Road, which becomes Birch Road.

23.0 Right on McCallum Road.

23.8 Left on Hardy Road and retrace your outward route to Harrison via Hwy 9, McPherson Road and Eagle Street.

30.1 Lillooet Avenue, Harrison Hot Springs.

26   Seabird Island
Kent

Round trip	14.3 km (9 miles) or 19.9 km (12 1/2 miles) with optional side trip
Terrain	Paved roads; flat
Traffic volume	Low, except for Lougheed Highway (Hwy 7)
Allow	1 1/2 to 2 hours
Highlights	Maria Slough, wetlands, mountain views
Starting point	Seabird Island Road near the Community School
How to get there	From Lougheed Highway (Hwy 7) approximately 3 km east of Agassiz, turn left on Seabird Island Road.

East of Agassiz, the Lougheed Highway bisects Seabird Island, home of the Stó:lō Nation. Established in 1879, the reserve comprises farmland and wetlands lying between the Fraser River and Maria Slough. The enterprising Seabird Island Band operates a cattle ranch, a nut grove, a truck stop and café, as well as running their own community school. Cyclists on Seabird Island Road will most likely get a friendly wave from residents.

We highly recommend the side trip on Chaplin Road. This country lane winds through a flat, narrow valley between the slopes of Bear Mountain and wide, peaceful Maria Slough. Returning (the road ends at a farmyard), you'll have a grand view of Mount Cheam rising to 2100 metres above the valley.

Although we have not specified a picnic spot on this short ride, perhaps you'll discover a suitable place, or drop into the Seabird Island Café for refreshments.

Geese on Maria Slough

The Route

km **0.0** Seabird Island Road near the Community School.

0.9 Option: Left on Chaplin Road takes you along the north side of Maria Slough to a turnaround point at Riverwyk Farm. Otherwise

0.9 Continue on Seabird Island Road through the reservation. The road eventually becomes Wahleach Road.

8.1 Right onto Lougheed Highway.

10.8 Seabird Island Café on your right. Cycle behind the buildings to find Chowat Road. This road runs parallel to the highway and will take you past Seabird Island Community Centre to your starting point near the school.

14.3 Seabird Island Road.

27 Bradner–Mt. Lehman
Abbotsford

Round trip	35.2 km (22 miles)
Terrain	Paved roads and unpaved trail (a hybrid bike is best for this); some hills
Traffic volume	Low, except moderate on 58th Avenue
Allow	3 1/2 to 4 1/2 hours
Highlights	Quiet country roads, daffodil fields, Fraser River, mountain views, Matsqui Trail
Picnic spot	Riverbank at Glenmore Trailhead at 18.3 km
Starting point	The west side of 264th Street, immediately north of Hwy 1 overpass
How to get there	Leave Hwy 1 at exit 73 and drive north on 264th Street to the north end of the overpass. Park on the wide shoulder.

Some rollicking ups and downs take you over the rolling Bradner plateau, famous for its fields of tulips and daffodils. Flowers have been grown here since 1914, when the Fatkin family planted the first bulbs. A few years later, the first Bradner Flower Show was held—an annual festival that continues to this day, around Easter.

After a plunge down to prairie level you reach the Fraser River at Glenmore Trailhead, where a recent 3.5-kilometre extension of the Matsqui Trail heads west through Matsqui First Nation reserve lands. This is a challenging trail with a somewhat loose surface and many twists and turns. Ride carefully and be prepared to give way to hikers and horse riders.

As part of the Trans Canada Trail system, the Matsqui Trail is no doubt destined to link up with Landing Road Heritage Trail—a section not completed at the time of writing. Instead, you stay high above the Fraser River through Mount Lehman, enjoying fine views of the mountains north of Mission before picking up your outward route opposite Bradner General Store.

Ostrich farm

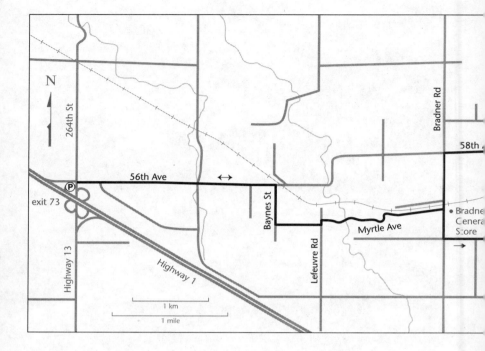

The Route

km 0.0 264th Street immediately north of the Hwy 1 overpass. East on 56th Avenue. This is a wide road through the industrial area.

2.8 Right on Baynes Street.

3.3 Left on Myrtle Avenue.

3.9 Left on Lefeuvre Road, then immediately right to continue on Myrtle. Caution: there is a steep winding descent followed by a right-hand bend and a sudden uphill.

5.7 Right on Bradner Road. The Bradner General Store is opposite.

6.2 Left on Haverman Road. Daffodil fields.

7.9 Right on Ross Road.

8.7 Left on Townshipline Road. Daffodil fields.

10.3 Left on Mount Lehman Road.

11.2 Right on Hawkins Road.

11.9 Right on Olund Road. There is a view of Matsqui Prairie before the descent.

Left on Bates Road.

14.6 Right on Townshipline Road.

16.2 Left on Glenmore Road. Cross Harris Road.

18.3 Cross the railway and ride to the end of Glenmore at the paint-daubed rocks. Glenmore Trailhead (information kiosk) on the right is a good picnic spot with a view across the Fraser River to Matsqui Island.

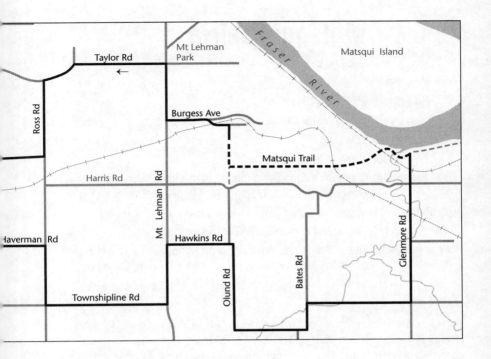

18.3 To continue, backtrack to the sign "Matsqui First Nation Reserve Lands" near the painted rocks. Go west on the Trans Canada Trail and follow signs for 3.5 km. This is a multi-use trail—please ride carefully and give way to walkers and horse riders.

21.8 Right at T-junction onto wood-chip trail and cross the log barrier. The trail rises steeply to join Olund Road.

Left at T-junction. Cross the railway tracks and keep left on Burgess Avenue.

23.1 Right on Mount Lehman Road.

24.0 Left on Taylor Road. Views of mountains to the north.

25.6 Left on Ross Road.

27.2 Right on 58th Avenue. Busy road.

28.8 Left on Bradner Road.

29.5 Right on Myrtle Avenue opposite Bradner General Store.

Retrace your outward route, jogging left on Lefeuvre Road to continue on Myrtle Avenue.

32.4 Right on Baynes Street.

Left on 56th Avenue.

35.2 Left on 264th Street to parking area.

28 Matsqui Prairie
Abbotsford

Round trip 25.2 km (15 3/4 miles)

Terrain Paved roads and gravel dyke path; flat

Traffic volume Low

Allow 2 1/2 to 3 1/2 hours

Highlights Clayburn Village Store, quiet country roads, berry farms, Fraser River views, Matsqui Trail Regional Park

Picnic spot Mission Bridge Picnic Area at 17.4 km

Starting point Parking lot opposite Clayburn Village Store

How to get there Leave Hwy 1 and drive north on Abbotsford-Mission Hwy 11, turn east on Clayburn Road and drive 2 km to Clayburn village.

Between the western base of Sumas Mountain and the Abbotsford-Mission Highway lies a pocket prairie. You'll cycle along quiet roads between berry patches and cornfields, fields of eggplants and red currants, past dairy farms, poultry barns, even an ostrich farm. In blueberry season, stylish scarecrows stand guard against raiding birds amid a cacophony of cannons and simulated hawk screams.

In due course your route joins the Matsqui Trail (now part of the Trans Canada Trail) along the south bank of the Fraser River. From the gravel dyke path you look out over riverside willows to Westminster Abbey, perched on Mission hill. The Mission Bridge Trailhead, our suggested picnic spot, offers an unusual view of the bridge as well as a spacious picnic area and other facilities.

Back at your starting point, tea with scones and Devonshire cream at the Clayburn Village Store and Tea Shop is not to be missed. This establishment, dating back to 1912, is a treasure house of special goods—Fraser Valley jams, Melton Mowbray pies, beeswax polish from Aldergrove, an entire wall of British sweets, and all manner of memorabilia from bowler hats to biscuit tins.

Before you load up your bike, take a ride around old Clayburn village. It is the site of a brick works, the Vancouver Fireclay Company, established in the early 1900s with the discovery of good fireclay on Sumas Mountain. Some of the company houses have been restored, as has the church, which was meticulously rebuilt brick by brick. And then there are the boutiques ...

Clayburn Village Store

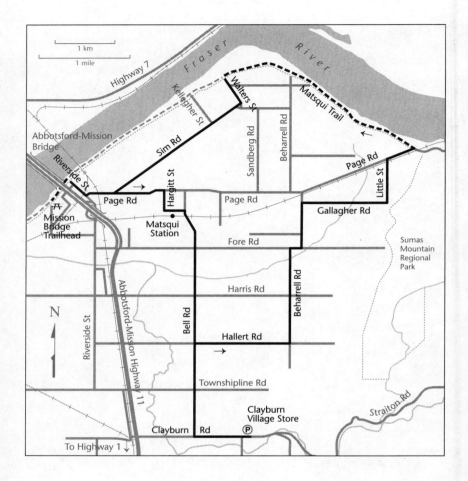

The Route

km 0.0 Clayburn Village Store. Go west on Clayburn Road.

1.0 Right on Bell Road. Blueberry farms.

Continue on Bell Road after the four-way stop.

2.6 Right on Hallert Road.

4.2 Left on Beharrell Road.

5.8 Right on Fore Road at the microwave tower.

6.0 Left on Beharrell Road. Watch for ostriches!

6.8 Right on Gallagher Road.

8.2 Left on Little Street.

8.9 Right on Page Road.

9.4 Left onto dyke path. Matsqui Trail Regional Park. Be prepared to share the trail with walkers and horseback riders.

11.9 Gate at the foot of Beharrell Road. Continue on the dyke path.

13.1 Another gate—go left here on the paved road (Walters Street).

13.5 Left on Sim Road.

16.2 Right on Page Road.

16.3 Right on Riverside Street. Cross railway tracks.

17.4 Left at top of road down to Mission Bridge Picnic Area.

17.4 South on Riverside Street.

18.0 Left on Page Road.

19.4 Right on Hargitt Street. Follow the paved road left before the railway tracks. Matsqui Station is on your right.

20.1 Right on Bell Road.

24.2 Left on Clayburn Road.

25.2 Parking lot opposite the Clayburn Village Store.

Stylish scarecrow

29 Sumas Prairie
Abbotsford

Round trip	40.2 km (25 miles)
Terrain	Paved roads and unpaved dyke; flat
Traffic volume	Low, except heavy around Whatcom Road overpass
Allow	3 1/2 to 5 hours
Highlights	Spacious farmland with mountain views, Sumas River, McDonald Park, McKay Creek Trail, fruit and vegetable stalls
Picnic spot	McDonald Park beside the Sumas River at 17.3 km
Starting point	Cole Road Rest Area
How to get there	Travelling east, leave Hwy 1 at exit 99 and follow signs to the rest area.

Most of us have gazed from the car at Sumas Prairie as we sped through the Fraser Valley on the freeway. This varied bicycle route takes you to some little-known corners of that flat expanse: a creekside trail through farmers' fields, a peaceful enclave in the lee of Vedder Mountain, 5 kilometres of flower-fringed dyke beside Sumas River, two inviting riverside parks. From every corner you can look up to the encircling mountains.

Once a 30,000-acre lake, the rich farmland between Hwy 1 and the U.S. border is the result of drainage and flood control measures during the 1920s. Today, well-kept farms, many with Dutch names, grow corn and other crops along with lush grass to feed their milk-producing Holstein herds.

Strong wind can be a force to contend with on this ride. For years we cycled the circuit anticlockwise and found ourselves beating against a head-wind along North Parallel Road at the end of the day. This new arrangement is kinder and you should finish the day more vitalized than tired from your prairie excursion.

McDonald Park picnic spot

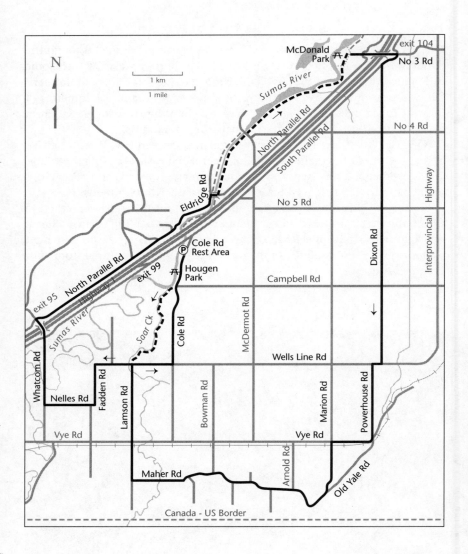

1 km
1 mile

exit 104

McDonald
Park

No 3 Rd

Sumas River

North Parallel Rd

South Parallel Rd

No 4 Rd

Eldridge Rd

No 5 Rd

Dixon Rd

Interprovincial Highway

Cole Rd
Rest Area

Hougen
Park

Campbell Rd

exit 95

North Parallel Rd

Highway 1

exit 99

Sumas River

Soar Ck

Cole Rd

McDermot Rd

Whatcom Rd

Fadden Rd

Nelles Rd

Lamson Rd

Bowman Rd

Wells Line Rd

Marion Rd

Powerhouse Rd

Vye Rd

Vye Rd

Maher Rd

Arnold Rd

Old Yale Rd

Canada - US Border

The Route

km **0.0** Cole Road Rest Area. South on Cole Road. Pass Hougen Park beside the Sumas River.

1.2 Right onto the dyke path along Saar Creek. Stay on the dyke as it intersects farm tracks. There is a huge old cherry tree on your left.

3.5 Right on Wells Line Road, which becomes Fadden Road.

5.0 Right on Nelles Road.

6.0 Right on Whatcom Road.

Cross Hwy 1 on the overpass. Use caution crossing three access ramps before turning onto North Parallel Road.

8.1 Right on North Parallel Road.

10.1 Pass Sumas Mountain Road on your left. North Parallel Road becomes Eldridge Road. The Sumas River is on your right.

12.6 Right on Atkinson Road and go across the bridge to the south side of the Sumas River.

Left onto the dyke path (McKay Creek Trail) at the gate.

14.3 Cross No. 4 Road at the bridge and continue on the dyke. Sumas Mountain bluffs are on your left.

17.3 McDonald Park. Picnic tables beside the river. Toilets near the parking lot.

17.3 Go east on No. 3 Road to cross Hwy 1 on the overpass. There are fruit and vegetables for sale at the yellow barn.

18.6 Right on South Parallel Road.

19.2 Left on Dixon Road.

25.6 Right on Wells Line Road.

25.9 Left on Powerhouse Road. The old powerhouse is visible ahead. Don't miss the Mootel and the Udder Barn!

27.4 Right on Vye Road.

28.2 Left on Marion Road.

29.2 Bear right on Old Yale Road, which becomes Maher Road.

33.7 Right on Lamson Road.

36.3 Right on Wells Line Road.

37.2 Left on Cole Road.

40.2 Cole Road Rest Area.

30 Vedder River
Chilliwack

Round trip	35.6 km (22 1/4 miles)
Terrain	Paved roads, unpaved dyke and trail; mostly flat
Traffic	Low, except in Yarrow and on Vedder Mountain Road
Allow	3 to 4 1/2 hours
Highlights	Vedder Canal, Vedder River Rotary Trail, farms, nut groves, flower farm and craft stores in Yarrow, antique farm machinery exhibition
Picnic spot	On Vedder River Rotary Trail after 22.4 km
Starting point	Chilliwack Visitor Information Centre, 44150 Luckakuck Way
How to get there	Leave Hwy 1 at exit 116 (Lickman Road) and follow signs to the Visitor Centre.

Following our route through rural Greendale and along the Vedder Canal dyke, you will soon arrive in the pleasing little town of Yarrow.

In the 1920s, after Sumas Lake was drained and the canal was built to prevent further flooding, the first Mennonite families came from Russia and other parts of Canada to farm this corner of the newly created prairie. Today, as well as being a farming centre, Yarrow lures visitors with antiques shops and artists' studios; nearby is a farm that specializes in flowers for drying and an apple orchard where 22 varieties grow on dwarf trees.

After skirting the base of Vedder Mountain, we meet the waterway again at Vedder Crossing, where the river flows under the bridge as the Chilliwack and flows out the other side as the Vedder—a rechristening that took place early in the last century when the water was diverted into a new channel. On the estimable Rotary Trail you cycle downstream beside an untamed river whose clear pools and whitewater runs are an angler's paradise. Rotary Trail users can enjoy the magnificent scenery and picnic at one of the benches or tables overlooking the river.

A final attraction on this interesting ride could be the exhibition of antique farm machinery, automobiles and steam engines at the Atchelitz Threshermen's site behind the Visitor Centre.

Peach Ponds sign

PEACH PONDS

THESE PONDS SUPPORT
COHO & STEELHEAD
JUVENILES.

THESE FISH LIVE IN THE
SYSTEM FOR UP TO TWO
YEARS BEFORE LEAVING
TO THE OCEAN IN APRIL,
MAY AND JUNE.

NO FISHING.

 Ministry of Fisheries and Oceans
Canada

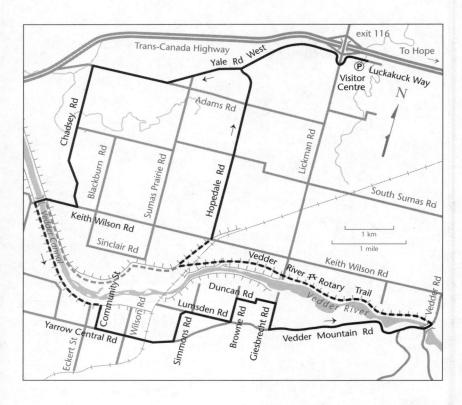

Resting on Vedder River Rotary Trail

The Route

km **0.0** Chilliwack Visitor Information Centre. Left (west) on Luckakuck Way.

0.6 Cross Lickman Road onto Yale Road. Pass the Chilliwack Golf and Country Club.

6.2 Left on Chadsey Road. Hazelnut groves.

9.3 Right on Keith Wilson Road.

10.2 Cross Vedder Canal bridge and descend to the dyke on the southwest bank.

13.1 Leave the dyke at the foot of Community Street in Yarrow. Watch for a narrow path descending near the community hall.

13.6 Left on Yarrow Central Road. There is a small park on the right.

15.2 Left on Simmons Road.

15.9 Right on Lumsden Road. There is a delightful backwater with stables and small farms.

16.9 Left on Browne Road.

17.4 Right on Duncan Road.

18.3 Right on Giesbrecht Road. Left goes to the Vedder Campground.

18.9 Left on Vedder Mountain Road. This is a winding road with ups and downs.

21.7 Straight on at the traffic light where Cultus Lake Road joins on right.

22.4 Cross the bridge over the Chilliwack/Vedder River and turn left immediately through the parking lot onto Vedder River Rotary Trail. Benches and occasional picnic tables. Pass Peach Ponds and Lickman Road access.

27.2 Cross the wooden bridge on your right and shortly after go right onto the gravel road, then left. Cross the railway tracks and proceed to the T-junction, where there is a Rotary Trail sign.

27.9 Right at T-junction.

28.8 Cross Keith Wilson Road and go straight ahead (north) on Hopedale Road.

32.7 Right on Yale Road West and retrace your outward route.

35.6 Chilliwack Visitor Information Centre, Luckakuck Way.

Columbia Valley

Fraser Valley Regional District

Round trip	11.3 km (7 miles) or 22.3 km (14 miles)
Terrain	Paved roads; some gentle hills
Traffic volume	Low
Allow	2 to 3 hours
Highlights	Peaceful countryside, pony farm, views across the U.S. border to International Ridge, historical plaque
Picnic spot and starting point	Columbia Valley Community Centre on Erho Road
How to get there	Leave Hwy 1 at exit 119 for Sardis and drive south following the signs to Cultus Lake. Continue on Columbia Valley Highway past Maple Bay and up the hill. Turn left on Kosikar Road and left to the community centre on Erho Road.

Tucked away at the foot of International Ridge is an Arcadian plateau. Since the region can be reached only by a long, steep climb from the south end of Cultus Lake, we prefer to transport our bikes to the top, contenting ourselves with an easy ride the whole family can enjoy. To make the most of this miniature Eden, we usually do the longer route, which includes an extra loop.

In the grounds of the community centre, a plaque honours early pioneers. Until 1916, when a wagon road to the Chilliwack Valley was made,

Spotted mare and foal

settlers in this valley had to cross the border into Washington to get supplies. Today as you cycle along the quiet roads, there is a sense of having fallen into a time warp: speckled hens scratch outside a cottage with beehives in the garden. sheep and donkeys watch you pass, ponies and their foals gather by the fence when you stop. Don't hurry or you'll break the spell.

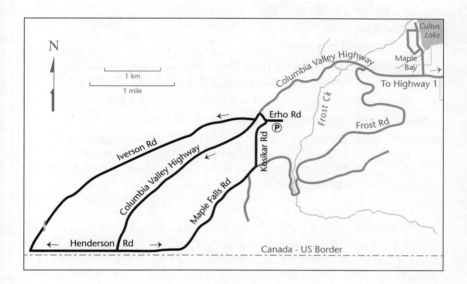

The Route

km 0.0 Columbia Valley Community Centre. Right on Kosikar Road.

0.2 Left on Columbia Valley Highway.

0.4 Right on Iverson Road at the fork. Easy rolling hills.

5.4 Iverson becomes Henderson Road on the bend. You're now cycling along the international border. A 12-metre-wide cut on the hillside opposite marks the boundary between the United States and Canada.

6.2 Henderson becomes Maple Falls Road.

10.3 Left on Kosikar Road.

11.3 Right is Erho Road and the community centre.

11.4 For longest ride, continue left on Columbia Valley Highway.

11.6 Left at fork. Columbia Valley Highway now passes through the centre of the valley.

15.3 Right and uphill on Henderson Road, which becomes Iverson Road.

21.9 Stay left on Iverson Road.

22.1 Right on Kosikar Road.

22.3 Left on Erho Road to Columbia Valley Community Centre.

32   Fraser River Islands
Chilliwack

Round trip	33.6 km (21 miles)
Terrain	Paved roads; flat
Traffic volume	Low
Allow	3 to 4 hours
Highlights	Camp Slough, Hope Slough, winding roads, farms, nut groves, mountain views, heritage building
Picnic spot	Kinsmen Park on Hope River Road at 19.7 km
Starting point	Rosedale Community Park on Old Yale Road
How to get there	Leave Hwy 1 at exit 135 and drive north on Agassiz-Rosedale Highway (Hwy 9). Turn left (west) on Yale Road East to Rosedale. The park is at the junction of Yale Road East and Old Yale Road.

Between Rosedale and Chilliwack, the Fraser River flood plain is laced with sloughs that effectively carve the land into islands. Cycling is the perfect mode of travel for exploring these meandering waterways. There's time to watch the herons fishing and the ducks dabbling in green, willow-fringed Camp Slough and to notice the overhanging walnut trees and the huge old maples. The Fraser River dykes, too, offer good cycling, but for comfort and variety of scenery our route follows the paved roads in their wanderings over Rosebank, Windermere and Fairfield Islands.

Having reached the more serious Hope River Road and rested on the banks of Hope Slough, you can enjoy an easy run back to Rosedale among a fair sampling of Chilliwack's nine hundred farms. Mount Cheam and its sister peaks dominate the scene.

Several historic buildings lie along your route. On Jesperson Road look for Jesperson House, built in 1912. Re-entering Rosedale on McGrath Road, you'll pass Rosedale Elementary School, a four-room schoolhouse erected in 1914, complete with a shed to house the horses ridden by the children to school. Rosedale United Church on Yale Road East was built in 1908 for a cost of $125; its original steeple bell is still in use.

Camp Slough

Goats posing

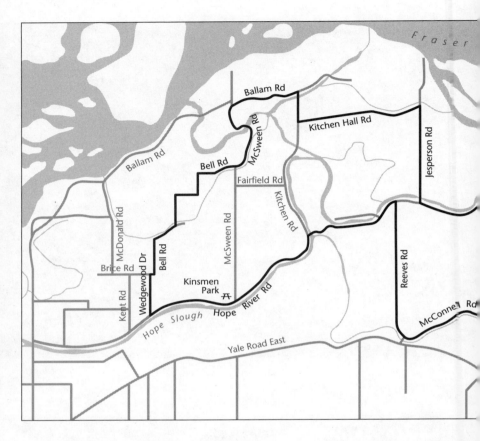

The Route

km 0.0 Rosedale Community Park. Right (north) on Old Yale Road.

0.8 Left on Bustin Road.

2.3 Left on Ferry Road. (Right goes to Ferry Island Provincial Park and Cheam Indian Reserve.) Ferry Road becomes Camp River Road. After passing Camp River Community Hall, watch for a row of heritage maple trees. Camp Slough is on your right.

9.9 Right on Jesperson Road. Cross Camp Slough.

11.3 Left on Kitchen Hall Road.

13.0 Right on Kitchen Road.

13.4 Left on Ballam Road.

14.3 Keep left on McSween Road where Ballam Road turns right.

15.7 Keep straight ahead on Bell Road. Enter the residential area. Jog right on Brice Road, then

18.2 Left on Wedgewood Drive.

18.8 Left on Hope River Road.

19.7 Kinsmen Hall and park on right. Picnic tables beside Hope Slough.

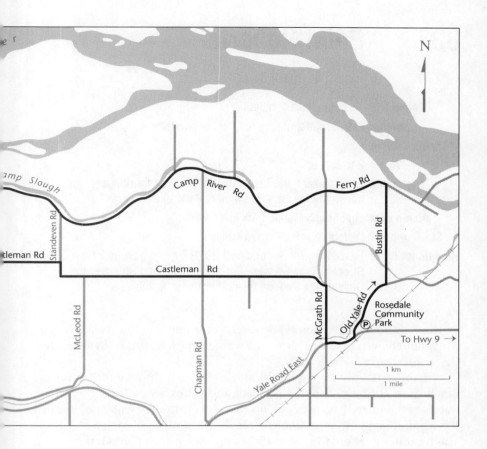

19.7 Continue east on Hope River Road.

21.4 Right on Camp River Road. Cross Gravelly Slough.

22.8 Right on Reeves Road.

24.8 Keep straight ahead on McConnell Road where Reeves bends right to meet Yale Road East.

26.4 Left on Gillanders Road.

Right on Castleman Road at the bend.

28.4 Right on Standeven Road.

Left on Castleman Road at the bend.

32.3 Right on McGrath Road.

33.1 Left on Yale Road East.

33.6 Left on Old Yale Road to the Rosedale Community Park.

33 Point Roberts
Delta/Whatcom County, U.S.

Round trip 16.8 km (10 1/2 miles)
Terrain Paved roads; mostly flat, one or two hills
Traffic volume Low
Allow 2 to 3 hours
Highlights Diefenbaker Park, Maple Beach, restored farmhouse, Lighthouse Marine Park, Monument Park, ocean views
Picnic spot Lighthouse Marine Park at 11.2 km
Starting point Diefenbaker Park, Tsawwassen
How to get there Leave Hwy 99 South at exit 28 (Hwy 17), then go left on 56th Street to Tsawwassen. Continue south on 56th Street to Diefenbaker Park on the corner of 1st Avenue.

Only a half hour's drive from Vancouver, Point Roberts offers rural cycling with enough ports of call to please the whole family. As this ride crosses the U.S. border, carry identification.

A flying start down Roosevelt Way will bring you within minutes to Maple Beach. It might be difficult to persuade the young set to leave the warm waters of Boundary Bay, but once on the road again they will enjoy seeing the windmill and old farm implements in the grounds of Maple Meadow. This beautifully restored 1910 farmhouse is now a bed and breakfast.

Having conquered the hill of the day, it's an easy run to Whatcom County's Lighthouse Marine Park at the southwest tip of the peninsula. Here you can explore rose-bordered trails among the sand dunes or enjoy a sheltered picnic on the boardwalk (leave your bikes below) or simply lean against driftwood on the beach and look out across the ruffled waters of the Strait of Georgia. Since strong currents and cold water are a deterrent to swimming here, you might be content to watch for pods of killer whales or sea lions—both frequently spotted from this shore. Binoculars could be handy. To learn more about marine life, visit the park's interpretive centre, Orca House.

Don't miss tiny Monument Park on your way back to the border. Here stands Boundary Marker No. 1, the first in the long line of Canada-U.S. border markers across the continent. The obelisk was made in Scotland; its history and that of the 1846 Treaty of Washington are inscribed upon it.

Back at your starting point, take a stroll or a rest in Diefenbaker Park, a green oasis created from a disused quarry.

Boundary Marker No. 1

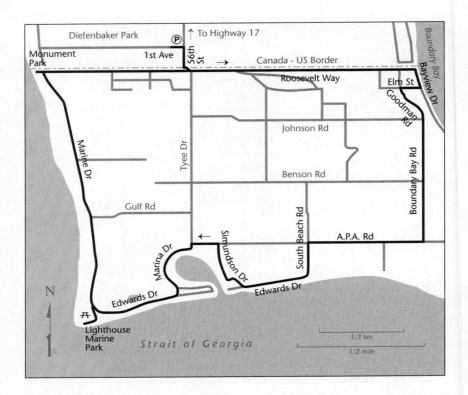

Diefenbaker Park
↑ To Highway 17
ⓟ
Monument Park
1st Ave
56th St →
Canada - US Border
Roosevelt Way
Elm St
Boundary Bay
Bayview Dr
Goodman Rd
Johnson Rd
Marine Dr
Tyee Dr
Benson Rd
Boundary Bay Rd
Gulf Rd
South Beach Rd
Simundson Dr
A.P.A. Rd
←
Marina Dr
Edwards Dr
Edwards Dr
N
Lighthouse Marine Park
Strait of Georgia
1/2 km
1/2 mile

The Route

km 0.0 Left on 1st Avenue from Diefenbaker Park.

Right on 56th Street.

0.4 American Customs. After checking in, backtrack to Roosevelt Way between American and Canadian Customs. Turn right, cross the Canada-bound traffic lanes, pass between the orange posts and continue east on Roosevelt Way. This is a long descent—use caution at road junctions.

2.9 Right on Bayview Drive in Maple Beach. View of Boundary Bay, Semiahmoo Peninsula and Mount Baker.

3.3 Right on Elm Street.

3.6 Bear left at Maple Meadow Bed and Breakfast. Restored farmhouse. Elm Street becomes Goodman Road. Begin climbing.

Goodman Road becomes Boundary Bay Road and levels off.

5.7 Right on A.P.A. Road. Left leads past a small cemetery to walking trails on Lily Point.

7.0 Left on South Beach Road.

7.4 Bear right on Edwards Drive. There is unofficial beach access at the foot of South

Heading for the beach

Beach Road—view across the Strait of Georgia to the San Juan Islands.

8.2 Edwards Drive becomes Simundson Drive.

8.9 Left on A.P.A. Road.

9.2 Left at the T-junction onto Marina Drive. The road curves around a sheltered marina.

10.2 Bear right onto Edwards Drive.

11.2 Left into Lighthouse Marine Park. Picnic tables, toilets, beach, camp sites.

11.2 Continue north on Marine Drive. Pass Point Roberts Golf and Country Club and the Roof House (famous for rich German cakes).

14.8 Monument Park. View of Tsawwassen ferry terminal and Roberts Bank coal port. At low tide look for herons in the shallows. Point Roberts is said to have the largest great blue heron colony in the Pacific Northwest.

Continue east on Roosevelt Way.

16.4 Join the traffic to pass through Canadian Customs.

Left on 1st Avenue.

16.8 Diefenbaker Park.

34 Birch Bay
Whatcom County, U.S.

Round trip 39 km (24 1/4 miles)

Terrain Paved roads; a few hills

Traffic volume Low to moderate

Allow 3 1/2 to 4 1/2 hours

Highlights Birch Bay State Park, Birch Bay beaches, ocean and mountain views, Semiahmoo County Park and Maritime Museum, Drayton Harbor, California Creek

Picnic spot Semiahmoo County Park at 15.8 km

Starting point Birch Bay Drive at the entrance to Birch Bay State Park

How to get there Cross the U.S. border on Hwy 99 (remember to carry identification) and follow Peace Portal Drive through Blaine. Continue south on SR 548 (Blaine Road) and turn right on Bay Road. Turn left on Jackson Road and right on Helweg Road into Birch Bay State Park. Drive through the park to the Birch Bay Drive entrance.

Does the mention of Birch Bay conjure up an unwanted vision of hot-dog stalls and summer cottages? If so, try this ride off-season when the long, empty beaches curve around the bay toward Birch Point at its northern end.

From there, all roads lead to Semiahmoo Spit, a windswept finger of land jutting into Semiahmoo Bay, much of it designated as county park.

The homeward leg of the ride offers a view of the North Cascade mountains and a spin through the forested state park.

The Route

km 0.0 Go right (north) on Birch Bay Drive. Beaches, cottages, stores, cafes.

2.7 Bear left on Birch Bay Drive. Cottonwood Beach.

6.2 Birch Bay Drive becomes Birch Point Road. After the residential park Birch Bay Village, begin a gradual climb, eventually entering the woods.

10.6 Birch Point Road becomes Semiahmoo Drive after rounding Birch Point.

15.0 Left at the stop sign onto Semiahmoo Parkway. Downhill.

15.8 Semiahmoo County Park. Maritime Museum on your left. Picnic tables and beach access.

Continue to the end of

Semiahmoo Spit (about 1.9 km) via the road or cycle path to the turnaround point at Semiahmoo resort and marina. Restaurants, stores, views.

15.8 Backtrack to the museum and begin a steep uphill.

20.5 Left on Drayton Harbor Road. Stay left where Shintaffer and Harborview Roads join. Begin a long downhill. Use caution as the road winds and narrows prior to crossing California Creek.

25.9 Right on Blaine Road (SR 548).

26.9 Go straight ahead on Loomis Trail Road immediately before the bridge. California Creek is on your right.

28.6 Right on Kickerville Road and cross the creek. This is a straight road with dips. Cross Birch Bay–Lynden Road. Cross the railway.

33.5 Right on Bay Road. Cross the railway again.

36.8 Left on Jackson Road.

37.3 Right on Helweg Road into Birch Bay State Park. There is a store on your right.

39.0 Park gate at Birch Bay Drive entrance.

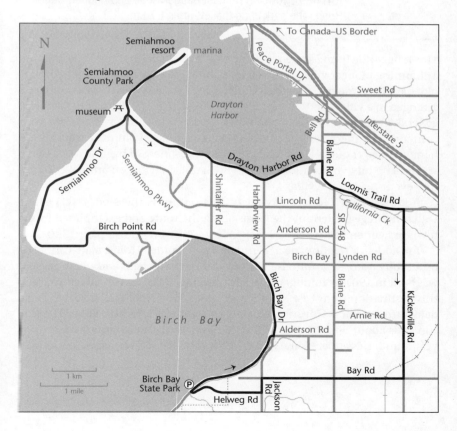

35   Nooksack Valley—Ferndale
Whatcom County, U.S.

Round trip 44.6 km (27 3/4 miles)

Terrain Paved roads; a few hills

Traffic volume Low, except in Lynden and Ferndale

Allow 3 1/2 to 4 1/2 hours

Highlights Dutch Village in Lynden, farms, orchards, views of Mount Baker, Pioneer Park in Ferndale

Picnic spot Pioneer Park at 22.6 km

Starting point Lynden City Park on Depot Road (3rd Street)

How to get there Cross the U.S. border on Hwy 13 (remember to carry identification) and continue south on Guide Meridian Road (SR 539). Turn left on East Badger Road and right on Depot Road. The park is on the left after 1.7 km.

This longer ride from Lynden into the Nooksack Valley has for its destination a charming pioneer village. Eleven log cabins, all more than a hundred years old, have been moved from their original sites around Whatcom County and arranged in a village setting beside the Nooksack River in Ferndale. A church, general store, post office, schoolhouse and several homes, complete with contents, are there for your inspection. Costumed volunteer staff are on hand to answer questions and add to the atmosphere of bygone days. If you visit in late July you can join in the Old Settlers' Picnic, an annual community event held in the village.

Adding to the pioneer flavour of this outing is the Nooksack Valley's Dutch heritage evident in the farms along the route and exemplified in the town of Lynden. (See the Nooksack Valley—Everson ride on page 132.)

An added attraction near Ferndale is Hovander Homestead Park. The beautifully restored farmhouse, surrounded by flower beds and a herb garden, was built in 1901 by immigrant Swedish architect, Hakan Hovander. To reach this destination from East Main Street (east of the Nooksack River) in Ferndale, turn south on Hovander Road then right onto Neilson Road. The side trip adds about 6 kilometres to the ride described. The county park is open year round; Hovander House is open Thursdays through Sundays in summer.

Entrance to Pioneer Park

Log Cabins, Pioneer Park

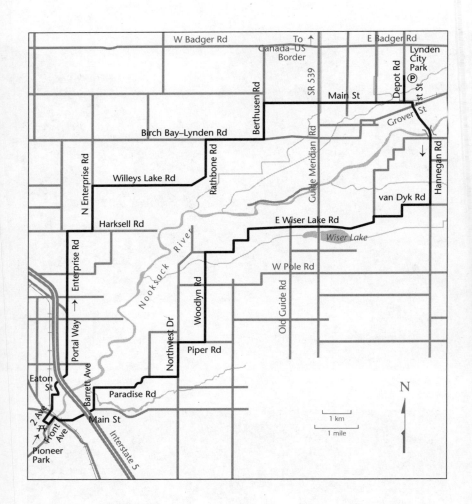

W Badger Rd · To ↑ Canada–US Border · E Badger Rd · Lynden City Park Ⓟ · Depot Rd · 1st St · Main St · Berthusen Rd · SR 539 · Grover St · Birch Bay–Lynden Rd · Guide Meridian Rd · Hannegan Rd · N Enterprise Rd · Rathbone Rd · Willeys Lake Rd · van Dyk Rd · Harksell Rd · Nooksack River · E Wiser Lake Rd · Wiser Lake · Enterprise Rd · W Pole Rd · Portal Way → · Woodlyn Rd · Old Guide Rd · Northwest Dr · Piper Rd · N · Barrett Ave · Eaton St · Paradise Rd · 1 km · 1 mile · 2 Ave · Main St · Front Ave · Pioneer Park · Interstate 5

The Route

km **0.0** Lynden City Park.

Left on 3rd Street (Depot Road).

0.6 Left on Main Street.

0.9 Right on 1st Street, which becomes Hannegan Road.

2.0 Go across the bridge over the Nooksack River and continue on Hannegan Road. You go uphill eventually.

4.7 Right on van Dyk Road.

Left on Huisman Road.

5.9 Right on East Wiser Lake Road. Winding road. Pass Wiser Lake on your left.

Cross SR 539 at the stop sign. Caution: very fast traffic.

12.4 Left on Woodlyn Road. Raspberry fields.

15.5 Right on Piper Road.

16.2 Left on Northwest Drive.

17.3 Right on Paradise Road. This is a winding road with ups and downs.

19.9 Left on Barrett Road.

20.8 Right on Main Street. Heavy traffic entering Ferndale.

Cross I5. Caution: very narrow shoulder for cyclists.

Go underneath the railway, then bear right and cross Nooksack River. Note sign: "Pioneer Park First Left."

22.3 Left on 1st Avenue.

22.6 Cherry Street. Pioneer Park ahead. Pioneer village, picnic tables, toilets.

22.6 Left on Cherry Street.

22.7 Right on 2nd Avenue.

23.0 Cross Main Street and continue on 2nd Avenue.

Right on Eaton Street.

23.9 Left on Portal Way.

24.4 Underpass to cross I5.

26.9 Straight ahead on Enterprise Road where Portal Way bends left.

Cross Grandview Road.

30.1 Right on Harksell Road.

30.7 Left on North Enterprise Road.

32.3 Right on Willeys Lake Road. Lake and orchards. The road becomes Rathbone Road.

37.1 Right on Birch Bay–Lynden Road.

38.8 Left on Berthusen Road.

40.0 Right on West Main Street.

Cross Guide Meridian Road (SR 539).

44.1 Left on 3rd Street (Depot Road).

44.6 Right into Lynden City Park.

Nooksack Valley—Everson

Whatcom County, U.S.

Round trip	27.7 km (17 1/4 miles)
Terrain	Paved roads; mostly flat
Traffic volume	Low, except moderate in Lynden and Everson
Allow	2 to 3 hours
Highlights	Dutch Village in Lynden, Pioneer Museum, Nooksack River, farms and country roads, views of Mount Baker, Fishtrap Creek
Picnic spot	Riverside Memorial Park in Everson at 13.1 km
Starting point	Lynden City Park on Depot Road (3rd Street)
How to get there	Cross the U.S border on Hwy 13 (remember to carry identification) and continue south on Guide Meridian Road (SR 539). Turn left on East Badger Road and right on Depot Road. The park is on the left after 1.7 km.

Lynden is such a delightful town that you may find it best, for the sake of the ride, to leave immediately by the back door and save the town's attractions for your return. Then you can stroll at leisure beneath the oak trees on Front Street, sample coffee and pastries in the Dutch Village or visit the Pioneer Museum to see a replica of a 1900s farmhouse and a collection of vintage cars and wagons.

The Nooksack River flood plain was dyked and settled by Dutch immigrant farmers. Today, as you cycle past the well-tended farms—many with Dutch names on their mailboxes—glossy Holstein cows raise their heads to watch you pass. At Everson, your turnaround point, the Nooksack River slides placidly past the cottonwoods at Riverside Park—unless you are there during spring run-off, when temporary fencing reminds you to stay well back from the swollen torrent.

The Route

km 0.0 Lynden City Park. Left on 3rd Street.

Cross Main Street.

0.7 Left on Grover Street.

Cross 1st Street at the four-way stop.

2.8 Right on Bradley Road. School on corner.

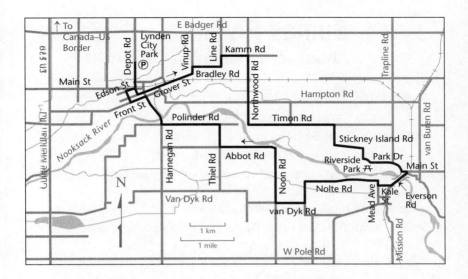

3.6 Left on Line Road.

4.0 Right on Kamm Road.

4.8 Right on Northwood Road.

Left on Timon Road.

9.8 Right on Stickney Island Road.

12.6 Stickney Island Road becomes Park Drive.

13.1 Right into Riverside Memorial Park. Picnic tables beside the Nooksack River, toilets.

13.2 Right on Park Drive, which becomes Main Street, entering Everson.

13.4 Right over bridge across Nooksack River. Use the sidewalk if traffic is heavy.

At the end of the bridge stay straight ahead onto Kale Road.

14.5 Right on Mead Avenue, which becomes Nolte Road.

17.7 Right on van Dyk Road (*not* straight on).

18.5 Right on Noon Road, which becomes Abbot Road. There is a good view of the river from the top of the embankment.

22.2 Right on Thiel Road.

23.1 Left on Polinder Road.

24.7 Right on Hannegan Road and over the bridge. Busy main road.

25.8 Left on Front Street. Busy intersection—it is best to walk your bike on the crosswalks. You are now entering the historic district of Lynden. Visit the Dutch Village and the Pioneer Museum at the corner of Front and 3rd Streets.

26.5 Right on 7th Street.

26.8 Right on Edson Street.

27.2 Right on Main Street, then immediately left on 3rd Street (Depot Road).

27.7 Right into Lynden City Park. Paths beside Fishtrap Creek.

37 Sumas River
Abbotsford/Whatcom County, U.S.

Round trip 39.8 km (24 3/4 miles)

Terrain Paved roads; mostly flat, some gentle hills

Traffic volume Low, except for Huntingdon-Sumas border crossing

Allow 3 1/2 to 4 1/2 hours

Highlights Farms, orchards, mountain views, Sumas River, Nooksack City Park

Picnic spot Nooksack City Park at 18.5 km

Starting point Vicinity of Upper Sumas Elementary School on Whatcom Road

How to get there Leave Hwy 1 at exit 95 and drive south on Whatcom Road to Vye Road. The school is on the corner. Please be considerate if parking during school time—there is plenty of space at the roadside.

Along this route, beginning on Sumas Prairie and continuing through the lush farmland in the shadow of Sumas Mountain in Whatcom County, you will cross the Sumas River several times. The wandering watercourse, however, is easily overlooked as it slips along between grassy banks and overhanging bushes. There are sequestered corners where gardens flourish around well-kept homes and wide views across fields of corn to the foothills of Mount Baker.

To the drivers of cars, trucks and milk tankers on State Route 9, the town of Nooksack is passed in a flash, but the cyclist notices the fine school on the hill, the homely post office building and the handsome sign announcing the city park. This sliver of land between road and railway offers picnic tables beneath a stand of beautiful Douglas-firs and maples. As this ride crosses the border, remember to carry identification.

Farmers' art

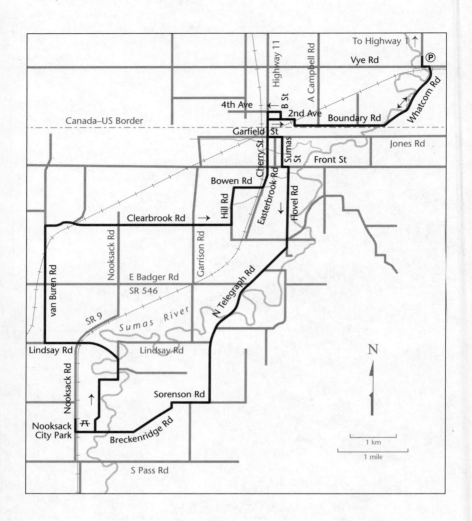

To Highway 1

Vye Rd

Highway 11

A Campbell Rd

B St

4th Ave

2nd Ave

Boundary Rd

Whatcom Rd

Canada–US Border

Garfield St

Jones Rd

Cherry St

Sumas St

Front St

Bowen Rd

Hill Rd

Easterbrook Rd

Hovel Rd

Clearbrook Rd

Garrison Rd

Nooksack Rd

van Buren Rd

E Badger Rd

SR 546

N Telegraph Rd

SR 9

Sumas River

Lindsay Rd

Lindsay Rd

Nooksack Rd

Sorenson Rd

Nooksack
City Park

Breckenridge Rd

S Pass Rd

N

1 km

1 mile

The Route

km **0.0** Upper Sumas Elementary School. Left (east) on Vye Road.

0.1 Right on Whatcom Road and cross the railway. The Sumas River is on your right. Whatcom Road becomes Boundary Road, then changes to 2nd Avenue at the bend by the lumber yard.

5.2 Right on B Street.

5.4 Left on 4th Avenue.

Left on Sumas Way (Hwy 11) to U.S. Customs. Enter the building and check in as a pedestrian before walking your bicycle past the booth.

5.2 Proceed south through Sumas on Cherry Street.

6.4 Left on Garfield Street.

6.5 Right on Sumas Street. The city park is on your right.

7.3 Left on Front Street.

7.7 Right on Hovel Road.

9.8 Straight ahead on N. Telegraph Road where Morgan Road intersects. You have glimpses of the Sumas River as you ride past dairy farms, eventually gaining height.

15.0 Right on Sorenson Road.

15.7 Left on Breckenridge Road. After a gradual descent, the road becomes Madison Street as it enters Nooksack.

18.3 Cross the railway tracks, then immediately go right on Nooksack Road (SR 9).

18.5 Right into Nooksack City Park. Picnic tables, toilets.

18.5 Backtrack left on Nooksack Road.

18.7 Left on Madison Street.

19.2 Left on 4th Street (Gilles Road). Pass an orchard of Jonagold apples on your right.

21.7 Left on Lindsay Road.

22.7 Cross the railway tracks, then Nooksack Road (SR 9) at the stop sign.

23.5 Right on van Buren Road.

Cross SR 546 (East Badger Road).

26.8 Right on Clearbrook Road. Winding road. Watch for decorative use of farm paraphernalia around the barn on your left.

31.0 Left on Hill Road.

Right on Bowen Road.

32.6 Left on Easterbrook Road, which becomes Cherry Street in Sumas. Proceed through Canadian Customs.

34.7 Right on 2nd Avenue.

Left on Boundary Road, which becomes Whatcom Road.

39.7 Left on Vye Road after the railway tracks.

39.8 Upper Sumas Elementary School.

38 Lower Samish Valley
Skagit County, U.S.

Round trip	33.9 km (21 miles)
Terrain	Paved roads; mostly flat
Traffic volume	Low
Allow	2 1/2 to 3 1/2 hours
Highlights	Quiet roads among farms, Samish River, Bay View State Park, Padilla Bay, artists' galleries in Edison
Picnic spot	Bay View State Park at 22.7 km
Starting point	Edison School Road, near Edison Café
How to get there	From State Route 11 (Chuckanut Drive) turn west on Bow Hill Road and drive 1.6 km to the Edison Café at Edison School Road. Or turn off Interstate 5 at exit 236 and proceed west on Bow Hill Road to Edison (about 6 km).

This easy, pastoral ride takes you through the heart of a fertile valley to the shores of Padilla Bay. Quiet roads unroll between fields of vegetables, grain, fruit and flowers. From its beginning in the Cascades foothills, the Samish River winds lazily across the plain to slide through estuarine marsh into Samish Bay. Below the bridge on Bay View–Edison Road you'll see tugs and gillnetters moored on the riverbank and ancient wrecks lying stranded in the mud at low tide.

From aptly named Farm-to-Market Road you'll descend to a beach picnic site at Bay View State Park, where you can look across Padilla Bay to March Point and Fidalgo Island beyond.

Take time to browse through the artists' galleries (open at weekends) in the quaint little town of Edison, or finish with coffee and pie in the friendly Edison Café.

High and dry beside Samish River

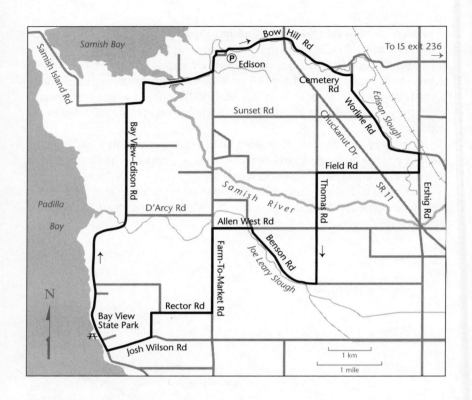

The Route

km **0.0** Edison Café. East on McTaggart Avenue, which becomes Bow Hill Road.

1.6 Cross SR 11 (Chuckanut Drive). The Rhododendron Café is on the corner. Continue on Bow Hill Road past the cheese stall on the left.

5.1 Right on Bow Cemetery Road. Some graves date back to the 1860s.

5.7 Right on Worline Road.

6.9 Keep right on Ershig Road. Dairy farms.

7.4 Right on Field Road.

3.0 Cross SR 11. Pass the quarter-horse ranch.

3.5 Left on Thomas Road. Cross Samish River.

11.1 Cross Allen West Road. Orchards and berry farms.

12.8 Right on Benson Road at the T-junction. Raspberry fields.

15.2 Left on Allen West Road.

16.2 Left on Farm-to-Market Road. Uphill!

18.7 Right on Rector Road.

20.9 Right on Josh Wilson Road.

22.0 Right on Bay View–Edison Road.

22.5 Right at the entrance to Bay View State Park, then first left through the underpass to the beach.

22.7 Beach picnic area. Tables, toilets, etc.

22.9 From the park entrance continue right (north) on Bay View–Edison Road. Gentle hills. Mount Baker is visible to the east.

30.3 Right at the T-junction. Samish Island Road goes left.

32.3 Bridge across Samish River. View downstream. Old and new boats are moored below the bridge.

33.0 Left on Farm-to-Market Road.

Turn right on McTaggart Avenue in Edison. Quaint buildings and artists' galleries.

33.9 Edison Café.

39   Padilla Bay
Skagit County, U.S.

Round trip 11 km (6 3/4 miles) including Bay View State Park beach
Terrain Paved road and gravel trail; one or two hills
Traffic Low
Allow 1 1/2 to 2 1/2 hours
Highlights Breazeale Interpretive Center, Bay View State Park, Padilla Bay Shore Trail
Picnic spot Bay View State Park beach picnic site at 10 km
Starting point Breazeale Interpretive Center
How to get there Leave Interstate 5 at exit 231 and drive west on Josh Wilson Road. Go right on Bay View–Edison Road for about 1.4 km to Breazeale Center.

Although Padilla Bay Shore Trail could be incorporated in our Lower Samish Valley route (see page 138), an unhurried visit to the Breazeale Interpretive Center before cycling the trail makes an enjoyable outing in its own right.

Padilla Bay is part of a National Estuarine Research Reserve. At the Breazeale Center, standing exhibits and saltwater aquaria demonstrate the life and importance of estuaries. Children especially will enjoy the hands-on room. The centre is open most days and includes an observation deck and a 1.3-kilometre walking trail through surrounding forest and meadow.

With this background under your belt you are ready to cycle the Shore Trail. Benches and interpretive panels add to the traveller's appreciation of the environment, which may be water or mudflats, depending on the tide.

At the Trailhead

Flanked by a tangle of beach pea and wild roses, the trail curves around the edge of the bay as far as Indian Slough. Beside this muddy channel it meanders inland to meet Bay View–Edison Road, giving the cyclist an optional return route. A picnic on the beach at the Bay View State Park rounds off the excursion perfectly.

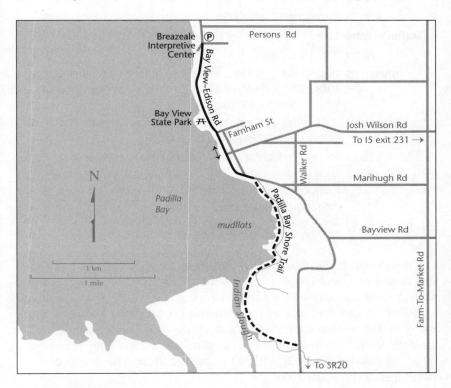

The Route

km 0.0 Breazeale Interpretive Center. Go south on Bay View–Edison Road. Pass Bay View State Park entrance on your left.

1.8 Right at the trailhead for Padilla Bay Shore Trail.

3.7 The trail enters Indian Slough and continues beside its north fork.

5.5 Gate at Bay View–Edison Road. If you don't want to return to Breazeale via the road, head back along the Shore Trail. For a picnic on the beach at Bay View State Park, turn right at the park entrance, then left through the underpass to the beach.

10.0 Bay View State Park beach picnic site.

11.0 Breazeale Interpretive Center.

40   Fir Island
Skagit County, U.S.

Round trip	39.3 km (24 1/2 miles)
Terrain	Paved roads; mostly flat
Traffic volume	Low
Allow	3 to 4 1/2 hours
Highlights	Pioneer Park, gracious old homes around La Conner, Dodge Valley, Skagit River, Fir Island farms, Fir-Conway Lutheran Church, Mann's Landing
Picnic spot	Best to buy lunch at the Rexville Grocery Store on Best Road, before or after exploring Fir Island
Starting point	Pioneer Park at the east end of the Rainbow Bridge in La Conner
How to get there	Go along Pioneer Parkway in La Conner toward the Rainbow Bridge and follow signs to Pioneer Park. The ride starts from the topmost parking area near the memorial plaque to Louisa Ann Conner.

The picturesque town of La Conner, while delighting visitors with its galleries and waterfront, also happens to be situated in easy cycling country. If you are staying in town and crave a break from shopping, why not ride out to Fir Island?

We've chosen Pioneer Park as our starting point partly because it is the site of an often-overlooked memorial to Louisa Ann Conner, whose initials gave the town its name. Also, from the park, you are soon out of town and wheeling through the Dodge Valley toward Rexville and the bridge over the north fork of the Skagit River.

Between the north and south forks of the river, Fir Island is an "island" of reclaimed land—flat, fertile and intensively farmed. High levees protect the area from seasonal flooding. Flat-bottomed steamboats once navigated the south fork of the Skagit River through its maze of estuarine channels (now a wildlife reserve) as far as Skagit City at the junction of the two forks. Nothing remains of that city now, but you will pass Mann's Landing, which was an important river stop along the way, and see historic Fir-Conway Lutheran Church rising from the fields in what was once the town of Fir.

Since Fir Island farmers use every inch of the ground for their corn and cabbages, and the river dyke bristles with No Trespassing signs, you may look in vain for a place to sit down and eat your lunch. We have a better idea: the Rexville Grocery Store on Best Road will be happy to make you a sandwich or serve you live Chuckanut oysters, to eat indoors or at their picnic tables outside.

Fir-Conway Lutheran Church

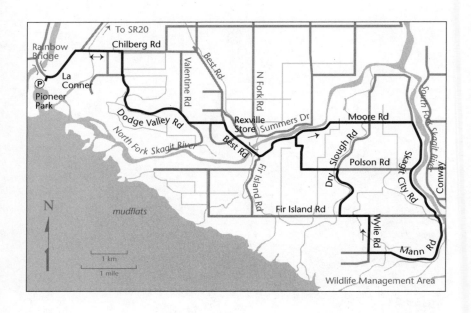

Rexville Grocery Store

The Route

km **0.0** Monument in Pioneer Park. Go right onto Pioneer Parkway and proceed along Maple Avenue.

1.6 Right on Morris Street. Straight ahead on Chilberg Road at the memorial.

2.9 Right on Dodge Valley Road. The road winds around the base of the hill.

5.5 Keep right on Dodge Valley Road where Valentine Road joins.

7.0 Keep left where Landing Road joins.

8.0 Right on Best Road.

8.7 Rexville Grocery Store is on your left. Go across the bridge over the Skagit River.

9.7 Left on Moore Road at the end of the bridge. View of Mount Baker.

11.0 Keep straight ahead on Moore Road where Polson Road joins. Moore Road turns inland and crosses Dry Slough Road.

14.5 Right on Skagit City Road.

18.3 Cross Fir Island Road onto Mann Road. Fir-Conway Lutheran Church is near the corner. The bridge over the south fork of the Skagit River leads to Conway.

21.8 Right on Wylie Road.

23.1 Left on Fir Island Road.

24.0 Right on Dry Slough Road.

26.0 Left on Polson Road.

28.3 Left on Moore Road.

29.6 Right over North Fork Bridge. The Rexville Grocery Store is after 1 km.

31.3 Left on Dodge Valley Road.

36.4 Left on Chilberg Road, which becomes Morris Street.

37.7 Left on Maple Avenue, which becomes Pioneer Parkway.

39.2 Left to Pioneer Park.

39.3 L. A. Conner monument.

Alphabetical Index

Index to Rides by Duration

Index to Rides by Distance